Tristan da Cunha

History   People   Language

Daniel Schreier &
Karen Lavarello–Schreier

© Battlebridge Publications
Box 421, 37 Store St, London WC1E 7QF, UK
Phone (+44) (0) 20 7278 1246; Fax (+44) (0) 20 7636 5550
e-mail <battlebridge@talk21.com>
website <www.battlebridge.com>

ISBN 1-903292-03-4

Cover design
Jeehoon Kim <jkim@synx.net>.

Cover photographs
Front (upper): Tristan's Peak (Daniel Schreier, 1999)
Front (lower): Tristanian men hauling in a traditional longboat in 1964
(Saint Louis University Archives)
Back: The Settlement seen from the crater of the volcano
which erupted in 1961 (Daniel Schreier, 2002)

Printing:
Latimer Trend & Company Ltd, Estover Rd, Plymouth PL6 7PY, UK

Table of Contents

To the Tristanians

In May 2001, the island of Tristan da Cunha was devastated by a hurricane.
The authors wish to state that all their profits from the sale of this book will go to helping
the Tristanians to repair the damage and rebuild their settlement.

Preface and

Acknowledgements

"Unusual" places like Tristan da Cunha attract considerable interest, and ours is not the first attempt to portray the unique and rich history of the community (for further information, we refer interested readers to the reference section at the end of the book). The present book, however, differs in one important aspect from all its predecessors: it was conceptualised and co–written by Karen Lavarello-Schreier, a native Tristanian who, now aged 25, spent the first 21 years of her life in the South Atlantic. Her co-author, Daniel Schreier, has a PhD in linguistics and spent six months on the island in 1999 in order to record and study the local dialect. To collect as much reliable information as possible, the authors conducted research on Tristan da Cunha, in South Africa, the United States, and Italy, and took many of the pictures in this book when revisiting the island in September 2002.[1] With the aim of presenting a picture of the community that is as accurate as possible, the Tristanians themselves were encouraged to read and comment on the manuscript, an opportunity which they had never been given before. The fact that the Tristanians added their own suggestions and insights is highly important to us, and it is our sincere hope that it results in the most authentic portrait of the people and life on Tristan da Cunha ever written.

The present book could not have been realised without the help of a large number of people who gave generously of their advice and assisted us in every possible way. We wish to thank James Glass, Chief Islander of Tristan da Cunha, who gave us permission to reprint his account of the 2001 hurricane, and who honoured us by writing the Foreword. An equally heartfelt thanks goes to the members of the Tristan community, too numerous to mention individually, who proof–read and commented on an earlier version of the manuscript. Their help and expertise was invaluable; it would simply not be a 'Tristan book' without it. Further, we acknowledge the support of the United States' National Science Foundation (grant BCS 9910224) and the William C Friday Endowment of North Carolina State University, for financing an important part of Daniel Schreier's linguistic research. We are especially grateful to: Philip Baker, of Battlebridge Publications, who believed in this book and published it, and from whose insightful editorial advice we benefited very much; Randy McGuire of St Louis University, who not only took great care of us while we were doing research in the archives of his university's Pius XII Memorial Library, but who also made available to us several of the pictures reproduced in this book; Marie Repetto and Brian Baldwin, who gave us permission to reprint photographs; the director and staff of the museum of local history in Camogli, Italy; and Walt Wolfram, whose incessant efforts toward proactive linguistic gratuity set such a wonderful example for us. We would also like to thank: Jean Swain and Anne Green for making invaluable documents available to us; Renée Green for her help with the Tristan recipes; Chris Willemse, Greg Ponticelli, and Helen Ponticelli for help with identifying Afrikaans words in Tristan da Cunha English; and Cynthia Green, for her help in collecting historical documents and photographs of Tristan. Last but not least, we are indebted to a number of friends who read and commented on the manuscript: Becky Childs, Bryan Cooke, Christine Mallinson, Jeffrey Reaser, Natalie Schilling-Estes, Shirley Willemse, and Laura Wright.

Daniel Schreier
Karen Lavarello-Schreier
Regensburg, Germany, June 2003

---

[1]   Details of the sources of the illustrations in this book will be found on the next page.

Illustrations

Battlebridge Publications is grateful to everyone who provided photographs and other illustrations for use in this book.

Credits and other details for the colour photographs on the front and back covers are given on page ii (above).

The sources of the black and white illustrations contained in the interior of this book are as follows (numbers refer to pages; location is indicated where there are two or more pictures on the same page):

Brian Baldwin: 3, 43 (upper).

Marie Repetto: 2, 33 (lower), 73, 74 (both).

The following images are used courtesy of the Saint Louis University Archives: 7, 11, 14, 15, 17 (all three), 18 (both), 19 (all four), 20, 23 (both), 24, 25, 26, 27 (both), 43 (lower).

Daniel Schreier [1999]: 32 (upper), 39, 41 (both), 42, 44, 45, 47 (upper), 48, 70 (middle and lower left).

Daniel Schreier [2002]: 30, 32 (lower), 33 (upper), 34, 35, 36, 38 (both), 46 (both), 47 (lower), 49, 57, 70 (all except middle and lower left), 71 (all six), 76.

Tristan da Cunha

South Atlantic Ocean

Foreword

I am delighted that this book is being published, and that I have been asked to contribute the foreword to a captivating and scholarly work about Tristan da Cunha. For the community and myself, it is very satisfying to know that this book was co-written by a Tristanian, whose insights contributed to make this a most accurate account of our life, history and cuisine (as I suspect the authors may have written this book partly for love of our traditional dishes like "tater" cakes and crawfish hash...). Also, the book reflects the changes on the island and provides an introduction to the island dialect, which at one time we feared would be lost.

It is very challenging for me to write a foreword to a book that has done our island justice for once. Tristan is an egalitarian society and the islanders are fiercely proud of their way of life, freedom and independence. Visitors to our island know how difficult it is to keep the right balance on Tristan, while outside there is a world that is constantly changing. While dealing with the limitations and advantages in a life of isolation, we Tristanians have always accepted this as a most vital part of our lifestyle. After all, life is more than making money. The many people who have lived and worked on our island know that once the peace and beauty of the islands get under your skin and reach inside you, they will remain with you forever.

Through this book the wider public has the opportunity to understand – and get a feeling of what life is like – on the world's most isolated inhabited island. It is only by improving our knowledge of the islands that we can ensure our unique dialect and preserve our history and culture, and this book makes an important contribution to the advancement of that understanding.

The community and myself would like to express our sincere thanks to the authors who have dedicated the proceeds of this book to the Tristan Disaster Fund.

James Glass
Chief Islander of Tristan da Cunha

Introduction

Tristan da Cunha, South Atlantic Ocean

According to the 1998 edition of the Guinness Book of Records, Tristan da Cunha, situated in the mid-central South Atlantic Ocean, is "the remotest inhabited island in the world". Situated approximately half way between Cape Town (South Africa) and Montevideo (Uruguay), the village in which the 285 islanders, who call themselves "Tristanians", live is 2,334 kilometres (or 1,450 miles) distant from the next permanently inhabited settlement: Jamestown, the capital of St Helena. St Helena, the former exile of Napoleon Bonaparte, is another island in the South Atlantic Ocean, further north and closer to the equator. The remoteness of the Tristan da Cunha community is truly unparalleled, particularly when put in context and illustrated with reference to well–known urban areas. In the United States, for instance, one would have to travel from Chicago to Miami just to get from one town to the next. The European equivalent of the distance between Tristan da Cunha and St Helena is a direct line from Frankfurt to Istanbul.

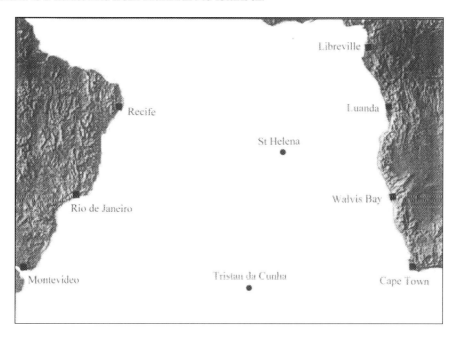

Planning a trip to the world's loneliest island requires time, meticulous planning and good nerves. Even though St Helena is the closest settlement, there is no direct connection between the two islands (unless travelling on a yacht). Anybody interested in visiting Tristan has first to fly to Cape Town, and then catch a ship from there. This considerably lengthens the journey: Cape Town is about 2,800 kilometres (1,750 miles) away, which is the equivalent of the distance between New York City and Denver (Colorado), or between Dublin and Moscow. To complicate travel plans still further, it is practically impossible to travel from South Africa to Tristan da Cunha on a date of one's own choosing. Visitors need a lot of patience and good timing because no more than eight to ten ships make the trip each year. A South African company sends fishing ships at irregular intervals, and a few cruise liners and an annual supply ship schedule trips to Tristan as well. The final

1

complication is that travelling from Cape Town to Tristan da Cunha may take anywhere between 5 and 14 days, depending on weather conditions that are always unpredictable and ever–changing.

Travelling to the world's loneliest island is a real experience. Visitors spend days on the open sea, seeing nothing but the deep blue of the water and the sky above. Along the South African coast numerous varieties of seabirds circle around the ship, but with every passing hour their numbers decrease and there are hardly any birds after about two to three days on the ship. Occasionally dolphins, whales or sunbathing sharks can be seen, but apart from that, the monotony of sea and sky prevails. Then, gradually, birds seem to appear out of nowhere and circle around in ever–increasing numbers – land must be near. Particularly impressive is the sight of gliding albatrosses; the effortlessness with which they move through the air is of unparalleled elegance and truly inspiring.

Then, all of a sudden, a dark mountain emerges, rising steeply from the depths of the sea. Visitors are overwhelmed by the impressions of this gigantic black cone in the sea, which contrasts so sharply with the monotony of the days on open sea. On a clear day the 'mountain in the sea', as some have described it, can be seen on the horizon from a distance of more than 150 kilometres. Black cliffs dominate the beach line and from afar the island looks virtually inaccessible.

A view of Tristan da Cunha in early spring, with the peak,
still snow-covered, emerging from the clouds

First-time visitors take some time to realise that Tristan is inhabited; they simply cannot imagine where a village might be situated. The steep cliffs, seemingly surrounding the island on all sides, give the impression that a landing is impossible, let alone that a permanent settlement might exist there. However, as the ship approaches the island and gets closer to the northern shore, a small plateau becomes visible and a number of houses can be discerned.

Edinburgh of the Seven Seas,
the island's only settlement which is home to 285 people

The next adventure is getting ashore. The little harbour is unsuitable for the off–loading of freight and passengers. The shallowest part of the harbour area is merely 40 centimetres deep, and this poses a real challenge for landing on the island. The only way to get ashore is a "taxi service", i.e. barges that transport people and cargo from the ships to the island. Visitors have to descend their ships on rope ladders, assisted by men on the barge, and are then transported to the island. If wind or weather prevents the off–loading, the ship has to wait in the lee of the island until the weather conditions improve. More than once has it happened that ships were forced to return to South Africa with all their cargo after a week of bad weather had made it impossible to take the supplies ashore.

The geophysical isolation, as well as the inaccessibility of the island, has had the consequence that relatively few outsiders have visited or stayed on Tristan. Tourism is in short supply, and visitors come to the island only on about two or three occasions a year (when the weather permits, that is), mostly on cruise ships. They usually stay for a day, wandering around the Settlement or daring to go hiking on the mountain, and then they return to the ship at dusk. The islanders guide tourists around the island, showing them the most spectacular views as well as the superb wildlife the island has to offer. The Tristanians usually look forward to having a chat with people from the outside world, but the visits have uncomfortable side effects also. Most importantly, the arrival of ships is very often accompanied by epidemics, since the local community is not immune to diseases brought by visitors. In 2000, for instance, tourists introduced a variety of whooping cough that troubled some Tristanians for more than four months. Older members of the community are particularly afraid of epidemics and are reluctant to leave their houses until the tourists have left and the ship has lifted anchor.

A number of outsiders, mostly from the UK or South Africa, live on Tristan for longer periods of time. They usually have an official mandate, mostly in political administration, medical care, or economic development. Until recently, a number of expatriates were employed as teachers or consultants, whereas others again are fascinated by the locality and come to live on the "world's loneliest island" for a while. The Tristanians have a special name for the people who come from the outside world to share their lives with them: they call them "station fellas". For most people, staying on Tristan is an unforgettable and once-in-a-lifetime event. Outsiders are most impressed by the rugged beauty of the island and its surroundings as well as by the generosity and friendliness of the community. Visitors quickly learn that geographical isolation has nothing to do with loneliness. Even though the comparative lack of contact with other people has at all times influenced the social history and the life of the islanders, the Tristanians are far from backward and self–centred loners (as some short–term visitors or journalists have wrongly assumed). After overcoming a short period of natural shyness towards outsiders, the Tristanians are keen to share their world with visitors and happy to introduce outsiders to their unique culture and lifestyle. Most "station fellas" leave Tristan with fond memories of their stay and return to the outside world with favourable impressions of the island.

Chapter 1

The history of Tristan da Cunha

The geographical location of Tristan da Cunha has had a profound impact on its history ever since it was discovered by the Portuguese in 1506. Being so remote and difficult to access, the island remained uninhabited for almost three centuries. Even though ships occasionally called at Tristan, the island only attracted visitors when the American fishing and whaling industry expanded to the South Atlantic Ocean in the late 18th century. Consequently, Tristan was not colonized until the founders of today's community arrived in 1816 to establish the first permanent settlement. With the exception of a two–year interval in the early 1960s, the island has been continuously inhabited ever since.

1.1 Discoverers, whalers, and adventurers (1506 – 1816)

In 1506, the Portuguese admiral Tristão da Cunha[1] sailed on the southern route from South America to Table Bay, South Africa. Being the leading sea power at that time, the Portuguese were the first to discover the trade winds that blew along the coast of Brazil and then across the South Atlantic to the Cape of Good Hope. On his first voyage on this unfamiliar route, Cunha erroneously sailed too far south. Several sailors in his fleet died of starvation or froze to death, being unprepared for the harsh climate and the freezing temperatures. The admiral then corrected the course of his ships and sailed northeast. By doing so, he discovered a hitherto unknown island in the middle of the South Atlantic Ocean – a huge volcanic cone that rose steeply from the bottom of the sea.

While it is still not clear whether the Portuguese ever set foot on Tristan or merely charted its position en route to the Indian Ocean, there is some evidence that they did land there. The first permanent inhabitants of the island, arriving in the early 19th century, found large numbers of wild goats and pigs. The presence of these animals suggests that members of Cunha's fleet, or other Portuguese sailors who followed in his wake, may have landed on the island. The Portuguese were the first maritime superpower and ventured to areas nobody had explored before. When discovering uninhabited places they considered of interest to their empire, they sometimes put goats or pigs ashore so that, if other ships were to call there later, there would be a source of food for their crews.

Despite the fact that no records of a landing are known, there is no doubt that the Portuguese developed an interest in Tristan and the other islands of this group. Tristan made its first appearance on nautical maps that were produced around 1509, under the inscription *ilhas que achou tristan da cunha* (word for word: islands / that / discovered / Tristan da Cunha). The islands were also shown in charts of 1520 and 1534, as well as on Mercator's world map of 1541. There is similarly no reliable information as to whether and when other Portuguese fleets were sent out to explore the islands. Official documents suggest that the Portuguese had no serious colonization plans, and it is fairly certain that the Tristan group was infrequently visited in the remainder of the 16th century.

The English and Dutch followed the Portuguese sailing routes in the early 17th century, and on the 25th September 1601, the Dutch vessel *Bruinvis*, bound from Amsterdam to the East Indies, anchored off the coast of Tristan da Cunha. The skipper reports their discovery of the island as follows:

---

[1]   The *nh* of *Cunha* is pronounced [ɲ] in Portuguese (somewhat like *ny* in *canyon*) but the Tristanians themselves always pronounce *Cunha* as [kunə].

5

On the 25th they came to the thirty–sixth degree, sailing eastward with a prevailing breeze by which they came to an island that they had not seen in the daytime... In the morning the ships came near the coast; it was a high one and as they could observe, a round island covered on the top with snow. Apparently there were no landing places owing to the steepness of the cliffs on all sides; in consequence they stood off again. Then they felt a great whirlwind rapidly coming down from the heights of the island.

On the 26th of the Autumn month Willem brought up a new topmast, the violent winds having long prevented this. Then the ships made for the land at the Cape of the Good Hope (Brander 1940:25).

The Dutch East India Company recognized that the voyages to the Dutch colonies on the Cape were considerably faster when ships took the southern route, picking up the westerly winds off the coast of Brazil and then sailing across the South Atlantic Ocean to Table Bay; consequently, in 1617 the directors of the company made the southern route mandatory for all commanders of vessels travelling to the Cape. Dutch logbooks from the 1620s and 1630s frequently mention Tristan da Cunha but attempts at landing (such as one in 1628) were not successful.

It was not until 1643 that sailors first set foot on Tristan. The Dutch vessel *Heemstede* anchored off Tristan for eight days, and its crew managed a landing on February 23. They reported that the ship "took in very good fresh water, while the crew was refreshed with vegetables, seamews, penguins, seals, and very good fish, which are to be found in surprising abundance" (Brander 1940:28). The favourable reports encouraged Jan van Riebeeck, the first governor of the Dutch colony at the Cape of Good Hope, to send out the galiot *t 'Nachtglas* in order to explore whether the island could be used as a refreshment and supply station for the Dutch fleet. However, the commander's report upon his return to the Cape was entirely unfavourable. After a second exploratory trip failed in 1669, the Dutch East India Company abandoned all colonization plans for Tristan da Cunha as well.

Of all the seafaring powers, it was the Dutch who were most interested in exploring the islands during this period. Albert Beintema, who conducted extensive research on shipping in the South Atlantic, notes:

We may well call the 17th century the "Dutch Period" in Tristan history. I know of at least 18 Dutch ships around Tristan or Gough during that period, against only six others (5 British, I French). By contrast, in the 18th century there were no Dutch visits at all. Tristan visitors were British, French (there even was an Austrian), and American.
<http://home.wxs.nl/~beintema/ships.htm>

The British were the last sea power to develop an interest in the South Atlantic Ocean. The first British logbook entry on Tristan da Cunha dates from as late as 1610. However, there were no attempts at settling until 1684 when the directors of the East India Company authorised three of their shipmasters to sail from St Helena to Tristan da Cunha in order to investigate the islands and to attempt a landing. The expedition met with no success for a most unexpected reason – briefly before the *Tonquin Merchant* was bound to set sail for the South Atlantic Ocean, the crew mutinied in the harbour of Jamestown, St Helena, capturing the ship and sailing off on their own, so that the captain had no other option than to return to England. When a second exploratory trip was not successful, the English abandoned their colonization plans. The island was deserted and remained unexplored until the end of the 18th century.

Even though the European seafaring powers had little interest in colonizing the island, their presence in this period left a permanent imprint – all the islands in the archipelago received names by 1700. The main island was originally charted by the Portuguese; then, however, the Dutch explored and named the other islands of the archipelago. These names changed again when the Dutch influence waned and the area was mainly frequented by the English and the French. In 1760, the English Captain Gamiel Nightingale visited the island known under the Dutch name *Gebroocken* ('broken') Island and renamed it 'Nightingale Island' in honour of his own name, as was the custom. In

1767, the French corvette *Étoile du Matin* landed on Nachtglas Island, renaming it 'Ile Inaccessible'. The islands' names consequently reflect the rich nautical tradition in the South Atlantic Ocean, and the islands in the Tristan archipelago bear names of three seafaring powers (Tristan da Cunha – Portuguese; Nightingale Island and Gough Island – English; Inaccessible Island – a translation of the French name), not to mention the now-abandoned names originally given by the Dutch.

In the second half of the 18th century, the relative quietness and solitude of the South Atlantic Ocean came to an abrupt end. The American fishing and whaling industry expanded southwards from the 1780s, and whale and seal hunters visited the area with increasing frequency. At least ten whaling ships, mostly from Massachusetts and New England, fished off the Tristan coast in summer 1789. The islands served as occasional resort to the sealers and whalers, and a certain Captain John Patten of Philadelphia stayed on Tristan da Cunha with a few men from August 1790 until April 1791. The men lived in tents on the north–western plateau and reported that they collected 5,600 sealskins during their seven-month stay. They claimed that they could have "loaded a whole ship with sea elephant oil in three weeks" (Brander 1940:50) if they had had sufficient manpower. Such reports did their share in boosting the whaling and sealing industry and attracted an ever–growing number of ships to the South Atlantic.

The growing economic interest, as well as the strategic position along a major sea–route, soon attracted adventurers who intended to settle Tristan da Cunha permanently. On December 27th 1810, a party of three men arrived on the island: Tomasso Corri from Livorno, Italy, a man named Williams, presumably an American, and the leader of the group, Jonathan Lambert of Salem, Massachusetts.

Jonathan Lambert

The main motivation of their settlement plan was to make profits by exploiting the natural resources of the islands and selling fresh provisions to passing ships. Lambert advertised his business in the *Boston Gazette* in 1811, publicly proclaiming himself as sole proprietor of the island group which he renamed 'Islands of Refreshment' (presumably for marketing and advertising purposes). In his newspaper advertisement, he encouraged:

> all those who may want refreshments to call at Reception [as Lambert had renamed Tristan da Cunha], whereby laying by, opposite the Cascade, they will be immediately visited by a Boat from the shore, and speedily supplied with such things as the Islands may produce, at a reasonable price (as cited by Crabb 1980:8).

However, Lambert's development scheme failed badly, and it took him only one year to change his mind. In 1812, he sent a message to the British government with a request to take over his property, on condition that he was employed on a regular basis and received a monthly income. He never received an answer. Lambert's plans and presence on the island were tragically short-lived: still waiting for a response from the Foreign Office, he died in 1812, for reasons that remain obscure. When the HMS *Semiramis* called in March 1813, Corri was the only inhabitant on Tristan da Cunha, claiming that Lambert and two other colleagues had drowned in a fishing accident. We will never know what exactly happened to Jonathan Lambert, but the people who met Corri in person soon suspected foul play and there were even allegations that he murdered his companions to get the full share of an alleged treasure.

The fate of Lambert remains unknown, but we do know that in August 1816, when serious settlement of the present-day community began, the island had just two permanent residents: Tomasso Corri and Bastiano Poncho Comilla,, a boy from the Spanish island of Minorca who must have arrived in 1814 or 1815.

1.2 Early settlement (1816 – 1857)

In 1816, the island was formally colonized, and it appears that there are two main reasons why the British Crown decided to install a military garrison on Tristan da Cunha. The first reason was strategic: during the Anglo-American war of 1812-14, American men-of-war and privateers attacked British vessels and they occasionally operated from Tristan da Cunha, using the island as a base camp for their manoeuvres. The raging war had serious implications for the little community, and Corri later claimed that American mercenaries repeatedly took away his livestock and produce, threatening to kill him if he resisted. This was a matter of some concern to the British Governors of the Cape colony, and they asked the Admiralty to consider annexation of the Tristan archipelago.

The second motive was by nature political and perhaps the principal reason for British involvement on Tristan da Cunha. Following the defeat at Waterloo in 1815, Napoleon Bonaparte was exiled in St Helena for the remainder of his life. The Admiralty was concerned that the French might attempt to bring him back to Europe and, in August 1816, the British Crown formally annexed Ascension Island and Tristan da Cunha. On November 28th 1816, an entire military garrison embarked for Tristan da Cunha, commanded by Josias Cloete. This comprised 5 officers, 3 non–commissioned officers, and 35 rank and file soldiers. Upon their arrival, they immediately established a settlement and a fort to defend the island in case of a military attack or invasion by Napoleon's allies. Tomasso Corri was overjoyed at the British presence; he assisted the soldiers in their work and helped them explore the island. He also boasted having a secret treasure on the island and rumours had it that he would sometimes disappear for short periods, only to return with gold coins to buy drinks in the garrison's canteen. Immediately rumours started that a heavy iron chest with incredible riches was hidden somewhere near the beach by a waterfall. Corri, in his desire for spirits, announced that he would show the secret biding place to his best friend, and the soldiers were only too keen to keep him company and to entice him to drink with them. We shall never know if there was any truth to Corri's claim, or if he simply took advantage of the soldiers' gullibility. However, we know that Corri literally drank himself to death and died of alcohol poisoning in early 1817, taking his secret to the grave. After he passed away, the soldiers started an immediate search of the island, but the treasure, if ever there was one, has not been found to the present day.

Meanwhile, the British Admiralty reassessed the situation and considered it rather unlikely that Napoleon's loyalists would ship the former emperor to an island that was positioned more than 2,300 kilometres to the south of St Helena. The admirals recognised that Tristan da Cunha was rather unsuitable for an escape route, particularly as Napoleon would have had to sail back north again, passing the place of exile on his way back to France. As a result, the Admiralty reconsidered the permanent settlement of Tristan. In May 1817, Lord Bathurst sent a letter Captain Cloete, informing him that it was "no more expedient to retain possession of the Island of Tristan da Cunha" (Brander 1940:84) and ordering a swift withdrawal of the garrison and all army personnel. The evacuation was substantially delayed and became a total disaster when the *Julia* shipwrecked on the north–western coast, taking down 55 men with her. The perilous Tristan waters have seen numerous shipwrecks, but this was by far the most fatal one.

It looked as if the island would be uninhabited once again, as the soldiers prepared to return to South Africa. However, just before the garrison was ultimately withdrawn in November 1817, a non–commissioned officer and two soldiers requested permission to stay on Tristan for good: Samuel Burnell and John Nankivel, two English stonemasons from Plymouth in Devon, and a Scottish corporal named William Glass, with his South

African wife and their two young children. Their request was granted and they were allowed to settle on and colonize the island. They used the buildings that were erected by the garrison and received animals, tools and plants from the soldiers who were leaving.

Still in the presence of the British officers, they laid the foundation of a joint project they called "the Firm". The men recognized William Glass as the leader of the community and devised their own constitution, formally decreeing that the coexistence of the community should be based on equality and cooperation of all its members.

Tristan da Cunha's original constitution

"We, the Undersigned, having entered into Co–Partnership on the Island of Tristan da Cunha, have voluntarily entered into the following agreement – Viz –

1st   That the stock and stores of every description in possession of the Firm shall be considered as belonging equally to each –

2nd   That whatever profit may arise from the concern shall be equally divided –

3rd   All purchases to be paid for equally by each –

4th   That in order to ensure the harmony of the Firm, No member shall assume any superiority whatsoever, but all to be considered as equal in every respect, each performing his proportion of labour, if not prevented by sickness –

5th   In case any of the members wish to leave the Island, a valuation of the property to be made by persons fixed upon, whose evaluation is to be considered as final –

6th   William Glass is not to incur any additional expence on account of his wife and children.

(Signed) Samuel Burnell
William Glass
John Nankivel[2]

Somerset Camp
Tristan da Cunha
7th November 1817

The community faced tremendous hardships and the first years were incredibly tough for the small colony. The men had to clear the land and make the pastures and fields arable (most of the plateau was covered in virtually impenetrable tussock grass). Fruit and vegetables had to be grown and harvested, and houses and huts had to be built and maintained. Glass's original plan was to barter surplus agricultural products for the bare necessities they could not produce themselves, such as flour, clothes, or coffee. However, his hopes were bitterly disappointed: the whaling and sealing industry was on the decline and only few ships visited the island in the 1820s.

However, despite the fact that the number of ships calling at the island was declining, a number of new settlers arrived and the population increased. The waters around Tristan have always been hazardous and wind and weather can change abruptly. Some captains underestimated how perilous the area was and there were so many shipwrecks that Tristan da Cunha became known as the "graveyard of the South Atlantic". As a result of these accidents, a number of shipwrecked sailors and castaways arrived. Some of them waited for the next ship to transport them to South America or Table Bay, while others stayed behind and added to the permanent population. Two more influential arrivals were Richard 'Old Dick' Riley (from Wapping, in the East End of London), who was

---

2   John Nankivel was illiterate and signed the document with a cross.

shipwrecked in December 1820, and Alexander Cotton (from Hull, Yorkshire), who arrived in 1821. Both of them settled permanently and lived on the island for almost 40 years.

The dwindling number of visiting ships was a matter of concern to Governor Glass and he finally decided to buy a schooner and export their products instead of selling them to passing ships. The plan was that crews of settlers should man the boat and export their products to the South African market. However, the enterprise was a commercial disaster. The first trips were not profitable and the endeavour came to an abrupt end when the schooner was wrecked in Table Bay in February 1823, apparently through carelessness of the crew. None of the ten deckhands returned to Tristan da Cunha. Glass and his remaining companions never heard from them again, and this added personal disappointment to financial loss. Moreover, Glass was bitterly disappointed when his comrade and co–founder Samuel Burnell was sent to Cape Town to sell sealskins and oil later that year. Instead of returning to share the profit, he spent the money on drink and eventually resettled in England.

An event of a different kind was to bring additional hardship to the community. In July 1821, the East Indiaman *Blendon Hall* was shipwrecked on the rocks of Inaccessible Island. The 50 survivors spent months on Inaccessible, living off raw fish, penguin eggs and muddy water before they finally managed to build a raft and sail to Tristan da Cunha, just 20 miles away. As soon as the people on Tristan learnt of the desperate situation, they set out to save the rest of the survivors and brought them back to their homes. But the unexpected presence of 50 people caused serious problems to the little community. Food supplies dwindled dramatically, and quarrels among passengers and crew led to social upheaval and unrest. When two months later a visiting captain finally agreed to transport the passengers of the *Blendon Hall* to Table Bay, all the supplies of the community were gone and they had to restart their efforts from scratch. Only two of the 50 visitors stayed behind, an Englishman named White and his wife Peggy (Lockhart 1933).

In March 1824, the *Duke of Gloucester* anchored off the coast of Tristan da Cunha to barter for fresh water and vegetables. One of the passengers was Augustus Earle, an artist and naturalist, who gladly took the opportunity to go ashore and make sketches of the island and its fauna. While he was painting on the island, the weather changed rapidly and a heavy gale sprang up, forcing the captain to set sail and take off. The poor man was left behind with nothing else than his painting materials and the clothes on his body. At first Earle was excited by the new surroundings and impressed by the friendliness of his hosts, who accepted him as a member of their community and helped him in whatever way they could. His initial excitement waned quickly, however. The months passed, no ships arrived, and he ended up spending more than nine months on Tristan da Cunha.

Fortunately for anybody interested in Tristan's earliest settlement period, Augustus Earle kept a diary of his experiences as a "castaway artist". His narrative is the first ever account of the Tristan community, and it provides fascinating insights into the harsh yet happy living conditions in the mid–1820s. He described William Glass and his companions as follows:

> The chief person of our little community (commonly called the Governor) is Mr. Glass, a Scotchman, a ci–devant corporal of the artillery drivers; and he certainly behaves to me with every possible kindness: nothing within his power is spared to make me comfortable. I experience from him attention and hospitality, such as rarely found in higher situations of life. (...) My three other companions have all been private seamen, who have remained here at different times in order to procure sea elephant oil and other oils, to barter with vessels touching here; and they all partake greatly of the honest roughness of British tars (...) Of the fair ladies of our colony, Mrs. Glass is a Cape creole, and Mrs White a half–cast Portuguese from Bombay. Children there are in abundance, all healthy and robust, and just one year older than another (...)
>
> Our governor, Glass, who is the original founder and first settler of this little society, was born in Roxburgh (...) The next in rank (for even here we must have distinctions

made) is a man of the name of Taylor,[3] and he, being the oldest sailor, steers the whale–boat; and, as is usual among all gangs of men engaged in either fishing, sealing, or any boating work of that description, those who are at the helm assume a superiority over their comrades (...) His comrade at the time I became a member of the society was a dapper little fellow, as Taylor used to say, "half sailor, half waterman, and half fisherman: born at Wapping, served his time in a Billingsgate boat, and occasionally vended sprats" (...) The name of this worthy was Richard, but he was always called Old Dick. He prided himself as being "a man–of–war's man", having at the close of the war entered the service, and was on board a ten gun brig; but every attempt he made at a nautical yarn was always instantly put a stop to by Old Taylor, with such epithets of contempt that he was obliged to desist; but his local knowledge of Deptford, Bugsby's Hole, the Pool, &c. was truly extraordinary (...) The last, and youngest of our party, is named White. There is nothing very particular in his history. He is an excellent specimen of a young sailor, has all and their characteristic warmth of feeling, and desperate courage, added to a simplicity almost childish (...) He was one of the crew of the "Blendenhall" Indiaman which was wrecked on a neighbouring island. He had formed an attachment to one of the servant girls on board (...) and he and his Peggy made the second couple married on the island, and no two people can be happier (Earle 1832).

Earle also described many of his adventures on the island, including hunting a wild boar and exploring the mountain. He returned the Tristanians' hospitality by helping out the community in whatever way he could. He acted as assistant minister to William Glass and as schoolmaster, helping him in his efforts to teach the children basic reading and writing. Earle also produced a number of sketches of the founders of the community, one of which is reproduced here, showing William Glass standing in front of his cottage.

In 1825, the first non anglophone settler arrived, a Dane named Peter Petersen, and he was joined by a certain George Pert (or Peart) who apparently fled from a ship to escape trial in New Zealand. The year 1826 saw relevant changes to the island community: The White family left Tristan da Cunha and resettled in the Cape area, and their departure was much lamented by William Glass. In November of that year, Thomas Swain, a sailor from Hastings, Sussex, arrived. In time he was to be another core member of the community and stayed on Tristan da Cunha until his death in 1863. Swain has an interesting story. He was a soldier in the English army but was taken as a prisoner of war by the French. They forced him to fight the British troops who in turn captured and kept him in captivity for years. They assumed him to be French, and he did not dare to reveal his true identity for fear of being sentenced as a turncoat. Swain had the reputation of being a great storyteller, and his ultimate claim to fame was that he served under Admiral Nelson and that he caught the dying admiral in his arms when he fell mortally in the battle at Trafalgar.

---

3   Earle is referring to Alexander Cotton, who, for reasons unknown to us, is sometimes referred to as Alexander Taylor.

The growth of the population had an important consequence as Tristan increasingly became an "island of men". Seafaring in those days was a man's world and women were not employed as sailors or deckhands. The community became increasingly unbalanced, as the new arrivals were exclusively male. In late 1826, there were at least seven men living on the island, and William Glass was the only one of them to have a wife and family. The islanders were obviously aware of their dilemma and consulted what to do. It so happened that the Norwegian captain Simon Amm called at the island to barter for provisions, and he knew the islanders well as he had called at Tristan da Cunha on previous voyages. The men talked to him and persuaded him to try to find female companions for them on the island of St Helena. There is some anecdotal evidence that the men offered him a sack of potatoes for every woman he would manage to bring along, but this story may be too good to be true. In any case, Captain Amm took this request to heart and on April 12th 1827, he arrived with several women who agreed to move and settle on Tristan. It is unfortunate that we know very little about them, but one of them had English parents and others were of mixed descent, and they brought several children with them. The arrival of the women from St Helena resulted in demographic balancing and led to rapid population growth. Governor Glass conducted a census in 1832 and reported that there were six couples – Glass, Riley, Cotton, Petersen, Peart and Swain – with 22 children.[4] Thus, the total population in the early 1830s numbered 34, which was quite an increase compared with the figure of 12 reported by Earle just 8 years earlier.

The 1830s and 1840s saw a revival of the whaling industry and numerous ships frequented Tristan da Cunha in need of fresh water and supplies. Indeed, the whaling was large–scale as Reverend William Taylor, who served as minister from 1851 to 1855, reported that as many as 60 to 70 ships were sighted whaling off the Tristan da Cunha coast at the same time (Taylor 1856). The increasing economic interest in the South Atlantic Ocean had consequences for the community. The most immediate one was the arrival of new settlers. When the *Emily* was shipwrecked in October 1836, Pieter Willem Groen from Katwijk, Holland, and Peter Møller from Denmark settled permanently, both marrying daughters of the women from St Helena. At the same time, the presence of large numbers of whaling ships led to the arrival of American whale catchers. Some of them were temporary residents and stayed only for a few weeks or months. Thomas Rogers, for instance, married one of Glass's daughters but left the island after two years. Other whalers settled more permanently: Samuel Johnson and William Daley stayed for 15 and 20 years respectively, and Captain Andrew Hagan arrived in 1849 and became a member of the community for almost half a century. Unfortunately, whaling had some negative effects for the community. Reverend Taylor reported that American whalers brought alcohol to the island and he was distraught because they apparently had a bad influence on some of the younger Tristanians. Another negative effect was the common practice of dumping frail or ill sailors who were no longer of use in the workforce. Glass himself wrote that sailors were repeatedly "left ashore sick from whale ships". The fate of most of them was a sad one. There was no doctor or hospital on the island and they received no medical care; some of them suffered for months before finally dying of consumption.

The re-establishment of the whaling industry further resulted in considerable out–migration. Whaling was a hazardous business in those days; whale catchers often perished during the voyages and the captains were in constant need of restocking their crews. As a result, young Tristanian men were offered employment on the whaling ships, particularly as they were expert fishermen with an excellent knowledge of the waters around Tristan da Cunha. Many of them accepted the job opportunities and left the islands for longer periods. Some Tristanians even left the island altogether. Five of Governor Glass's daughters married American whalers and emigrated to North America in the 1840s.

---

[4]   This census was discovered in a family Bible of descendants of the Glass family who later emigrated to America.

The year 1851 saw the first resident clergyman on the island, Reverend W Taylor. He served as a priest and schoolteacher and was assisted by one of the daughters of 'Old Dick' Riley and his St Helenian wife. Taylor sent letters and reports to the Society for the Propagation of the Gospel which offer fascinating insights into life on Tristan in the 1850s (Taylor 1856). Another very interesting account of the Tristan community in the early 1850s comes from Captain Denham, who commanded the RMS *Herald* and visited Tristan da Cunha on November 11th 1852. His reports show how strong the British character of the community was at the time: "The fine, healthy, and robust fellows, clad and speaking as Englishmen, gave the impression that they were from an island of Great Britain; even the Dutchman had become English" (as cited by Brander 1940:149).

On November 24th 1853, just two weeks after Captain Denham's visit, Governor William Glass, the well–respected patriarch and founder of the community, passed away at the age of 66 years, having suffered from cancer of the lower lip and chin for some time. Glass's death was much lamented by everyone who knew him. He left his wife and sixteen children, nine of whom were still living on the island. His death had considerable consequences for the community. In January 1856, Maria Glass, together with 24 children and grandchildren, left Tristan to rejoin their relatives in New Bedford, Massachusetts. When the archbishop of Cape Town, Dr Gray (to whose diocese Tristan da Cunha belonged at the time), heard of the imminent exodus, he sailed to the island to offer the Tristanians free passage to South Africa and resettlement in the Cape area. Reverend Taylor strongly advocated a total evacuation of the island population. Originally he had been supportive of the colony, but five years in geographical isolation turned him into a deeply pessimistic and depressed man. He saw no future for the community and persuaded a number of families to accept Dr Gray's offer to leave the island. In March 1857, a total of 45 people left the island, namely: William Taylor, the entire families of 'Old Dick' Riley, Peter Møller, and William Daley, as well as three daughters of Thomas Swain, three of Alexander Cotton, and two of Pieter Groen. Just four families, or 28 people altogether, decided to remain on the island: the families of Thomas Swain, Alexander Cotton, Pieter Groen and Andrew Hagan. There was nothing like home for them, and they could not imagine life anywhere else.

Therefore, the year 1857 marks a milestone in the social history of Tristan da Cunha. After almost 40 years, the period of Governor William Glass came to an end (and with him the early settlement period). The name Glass disappeared from the island for almost ten years until Thomas Glass returned in 1866. He married one of Thomas Swain's daughters and thus reintroduced the name Glass to the list of island families.

1.3 Isolation and growth (1857 - 1885)

The death of William Glass caused some social restructuring in the community, and Pieter Groen (or rather Peter Green, for he anglicized his name in that period) emerged as the strong man on the island in the late 1850s. When ships called on the island, it was Peter Green who would negotiate and barter on behalf of the entire community. He was a kind, generous, and intelligent man, and highly respected by the other members of the community. Douglas Gane, an English businessman who met Green when visiting the island in July 1884, describes him as follows (Gane 1928:24ff):

> He was a veritable fund of good humour and he quickly sought the Captain and made his own bargains on behalf of the community, giving lifestock consisting of diminutive pigs and sheep, geese, bluefish, crawfish and potatoes, which they had brought with them, in exchange for flour, peas, oatmeal, biscuits, cocoa, coffee and spirits (…). Peter Green became the "grand old man" in every sense of the phrase. He had married a native of St Helena who had proved a brave and in every way suitable helpmate. Such was his fairness and impartiality in settling questions that he acquired a great influence there, for he had a philosophic way with him that was most convincing (…). He is a man of education, with a gifted pen and irresistible humour.

Peter Green (Pieter Groen)

When His Royal Highness Prince Alfred, Duke of Edinburgh, paid a visit to Tristan in 1867, Peter Green acted as spokesperson on behalf of the entire community. Despite the fact that he officially represented Tristan da Cunha, Green impressed the Duke by stressing that the community had no elected leader, uttering the memorable words "I am in no respect superior to the others – on Tristan we are all equal" (Gane 1928). Green guided the royal visitor through the village when he paid a formal visit to the island families. Later that day, Duke Alfred was invited for dinner in Green's house and received a rare treat, a delicious island meal and the only bottle of wine on Tristan da Cunha!

From the 1860s onwards, the community underwent a period of growing isolation. The American whale trade had reached its climax in the 1840s and 1850s and declined quickly in the second half of the century; the increasing use of steam ships made bartering unnecessary; and the opening of the Suez Canal in 1869 drastically reduced the number of ships in the South Atlantic. All this led to decreasing contacts with passing ships. In the mid-1880s, for instance, the island was virtually cut off from the outside world; only about two ships called at Tristan da Cunha per year.

However, this period also saw important changes concerning the status of Tristan. The withdrawal of the garrison in 1817 put an end to the British annexation. As a result, Tristan had no official status in the Empire; even though the Tristanians considered themselves British and hoisted the Union Jack whenever foreign ships came in sight, they were not incorporated in the British Empire. This had consequences and a number of distressing incidents occurred during the American civil war, when American warships were engaged in sea battles around Tristan da Cunha. The most serious incident occurred when a confederate ship dumped 28 prisoners of war on the island after no proof of a British status could be given to its commander. When being informed of the incident, the British Government took the matter seriously and representatives looked into the matter. They discovered that the island had never been officially put under the protection and jurisdiction of the British Crown, and so Tristan da Cunha was formally declared a dependency of the British Empire in 1875. The colonial status was important as it meant that Tristan da Cunha was frequented at least once a year by one of Her Majesty's ships.

The Reverend Erwin H Dodgson, brother of Lewis Carroll, the author of *Alice in Wonderland*, served on Tristan as a minister from 1881 to 1884. He conducted a population census and found that there were more than one hundred people living on the island. His two major concerns were the construction of a church – up until then the community had

14

worshipped in the living room of Peter Green's house – and the establishment of an education system. Until Dodgson's arrival, Peter Green and one of Alexander Cotton's daughters had made considerable efforts to teach basic writing and reading skills even though they were not teachers by profession. It quickly turned out that, like Reverend Taylor in the 1850s, Erwin Dodgson was not capable of adapting to life in such a remote place. He suffered from depression and his physical health fared badly. His first reports had been utterly favourable and he was particularly impressed by the friendliness and helpfulness of the community. However, his initial optimism waned rapidly and he too turned against the idea of a permanent settlement on Tristan. In a letter to the Society for the Propagation of the Gospel, he deplored the "mindlessness of the children and young people and also of the grown–up people", adding: "there is not the slightest reason for this island to be inhabited at all. It has been my daily prayer that God would open up some way for us all to leave the island" (Evans 1994:254). It is not known exactly why he so desperately hoped that the Tristanians would leave their homes for good, but it seems that part of his frustration was due to the fact that the local men were simply too busy to be mobilized for the construction of a church.

| W F Taylor | E H Dodgson | J G Barrow |

The first three clergymen sent by the Society for
the Propagation of the Gospel to serve on Tristan da Cunha

Dodgson became increasingly frustrated. He failed to persuade the Tristanians to leave their island, and could not understand why they rejected the idea of resettlement in the Cape Town area. The situation culminated briefly before his departure in 1884, when he wrote a pamphlet, *About us Sinners at Tristan*, in which he referred to the Tristanians as a "new link in the Darwinian Chain between Man and Ape" (Evans 1994:254). His flock, needless to say, was bitterly disappointed when the pamphlet was found, and the Tristanians felt that they had been betrayed by a man from the outside world for whom they had had high respect. Peter Green expressed his disappointment by sending an official complaint to the Lords' Commissioners of the Admiralty; however, he did not lose his good sense of humour as he wrote that "if his theory about apes is true, we may say eat, drink and be merry, for to–morrow we will be apes".

However, the disappointment caused by Dodgson's cynicism was dwarfed by the community's most disastrous tragedy ever – a lifeboat disaster in which 15 local men perished. It is still not known why virtually all of the community's able–bodied men ventured out in one lifeboat to intercept a passing ship, and why they rowed out nine miles leeward in hazardous weather conditions. Perhaps the infestation of rats in 1882 led to a potato shortage, or all hands were needed as the men were unfamiliar with the handling of a modern lifeboat (which had been given to the community only one year earlier). We will never know what really happened, but the sad fact is that none of the 15 men returned. Rumours persist to the present day; the captain of the ship and Peter Green produced different (and to some extent contradictory) accounts of the event. Today some say that the captain and crew of the ship were careless, ignoring the distress signals sent by the men in the lifeboat, whereas others believe that the Tristan men were shanghaied and sold into slavery.

The lifeboat disaster was a terrible loss and inflicted an almost fatal blow to the community. Deprived of their husbands, Tristan became known as the "Island of Widows". When the *City of Sparta* called at Tristan da Cunha on December 26 1885, the total population consisted of 92 inhabitants, with just four married couples. There were merely four adult men on the island, Peter Green, aged 77, Andrew Hagan, aged 69, and the youngest adult man was Thomas Swain at the age of 45 – the rest were women and young children! News of the tragedy reached the outside world and Reverend Dodgson returned from England to offer his assistance. The British Government decided to send out annual supply ships to help the community. Again the islanders were offered a free passage to Cape Town and again they rejected the idea of leaving their homes. However, Reverend Dodgson managed to persuade ten people to leave the island when he returned in 1889. The population reached a low of 50 when 13 more Tristanians emigrated in 1892, and future prospects for the community were bleak.

1.4 Restructuring and modernization (1885 – 1961)

The late 1880s and 1890s were without any doubt one of the hardest and most demanding periods in the history of the Tristan community. The terrible loss of virtually the entire male population affected the community, and the women and children endured years of physical strain and emotional distress. They had to run the island alone and do all the men's work. They had to till the ground, harvest the potatoes, fish, and slaughter cattle – all the hard physical labour their husbands would have done. It is remarkable that the community was able to recover from this disaster. In retrospect, the will to survive and the decision to continue colonization against all odds attest to the strong character of the Tristanians. The way they coped with this terrible blow is the most remarkable testimony of their attachment to the South Atlantic Ocean.

The women and children did eventually receive a bit of help. The *Allenshaw* was ship-wrecked on the island in 1892 and the surviving crewmembers were forced to spend months waiting for the next ship. One of the survivors, Captain Cartwright, reports that he and his shipmates helped the community, and that they worked in the potato patches to assist the women. Cartwright himself fell in love with an island woman and stayed on the island for five years. He kept a diary of his stay and wrote that they produced their own food, living off fish, sheep, cattle, birds, and milk products.[5] A second fortunate circumstance was that two new settlers arrived when the barque *Italia* was stranded on the east coast of Tristan da Cunha in October 1892. Two members of the crew, Andrea Repetto and Gaetano Lavarello, both natives of Camogli, a fishing village south of Genoa in Italy, stayed behind, adding their names to the list of island families. As a result, the population started to grow again and an 1899 census revealed that there were 18 families with a total of 74 people.

---

[5] We wish to thank Anne Green of Tristan da Cunha, who brought Captain Cartwright's hitherto unpublished diary to our attention.

Men of Tristan – 1908
(On the middle row, Gaetano Lavarello is second from
the left while Andrea Repetto is on the far right)

Gaetano Lavarello in 1947
(after 55 years as
a Tristan resident)

The early years of the 20th century saw the deaths of some of the most influential members of the community. The first founding figure of the community to pass away was Mary Green, who had emigrated from St Helena to Tristan da Cunha as a young girl in 1827 and had been married to Peter Green for 65 years. Her death was followed by Captain Andrew Hagan, who had lived in the community for almost 50 years, and finally by Peter Green himself, who passed away in 1902, at the age of 94. Within less than two years, Tristan da Cunha lost three of its members who had influenced the community during most of the 19th century.

Shortly before his death, Peter Green had written a letter to the secretary of the Society for the Propagation of the Gospel (SPG), explaining the urgent need to have a resident priest and schoolteacher. This request was not immediately taken up – the Boer War preoccupied the British and South African governments – and it was not until Andrea Repetto sent another plea on behalf of the community that the SPG decided to send out a new minister. On 8 April 1906, fifteen years after the second departure of Erwin Dodgson, Reverend J G Barrow arrived with his wife and a servant to serve as missionary for a three–year term. They were joined by Mr Keytel, a businessman from South Africa, who was sent out by his company to start a local fishing industry. The first business scheme of Tristan da Cunha turned out to be a total failure: even though fish were plentiful in Tristan's waters, most of the catch rotted during the drying process and what was left was damaged by flies. The islanders could not attend to the produce all the time – they were simply too busy supporting themselves and had no time to export goods for the South African market as well. When the export of sheep failed also, Mr Keytel was forced to return to the Cape after only one year.

A traditional Tristan house, thatched with New Zealand flax

After the departure of the Barrow family in 1909, the Tristan community was almost completely isolated for more than a decade. World War I took the world's attention, the British Admiralty decided to abandon the costly practice of sending out an annual supply ship, and very few other ships called at Tristan at that time. The community received no mail for ten years, and at one stage they had no communication whatsoever with the outside world for more than three years. As a result, we know almost nothing about Tristan during this period, and it was only in the 1920s that ships called at Tristan again on a regular basis.

More information became available when the Reverend and Mrs Rogers served on Tristan da Cunha from 1922 to 1925. Reverend Rogers was concerned about the safety of his young wife and he enquired of the Colonial Office whether, in addition to his official function as a missionary, he could also be appointed resident magistrate by the British Government. His request was granted by Winston Churchill, who at the time was Colonial Secretary in Downing Street. The arrival of Reverend Rogers thus marked the beginning of a new era on Tristan da Cunha, namely one of a resident administrator with official status to act on behalf of the British Government. Reverend Rogers took the matter very seriously and started what he called the "Island Council", which consisted of the head of each family and the Reverend himself. Both he and his wife were very popular in the local community. They initiated a number of social changes, such as setting up a Boy Scouts group and teaching the younger generation football and cricket. In a letter to a friend in England, one of the islanders wrote in 1923: "I am sure the children shall miss the Reverend Rogers for they love him very much (...). It is the first time that they have seen a football" (Evans 1994:264).

Tristan schoolchildren in 1923

Offloading goods (1923)

The extent of Tristan da Cunha's isolation in the late 1920s is illustrated well in a letter written by one of the successors of the Rogers, Philip Lindsay. He was sent to the island in 1925, and – like many of his predecessors – he suffered from depression and illness. In 1929, he bitterly complained to the Society for the Propagation of the Gospel:

> It is alarming to realise that not a single cargo vessel has called here on its own account since 1925 (3 years). How can we get back under such conditions? If one calls it may not take us. We have seen no trace of a ship in nearly a year!! We cannot stand this much longer. – I am not too well – my teeth are aching. What shall we do. PLEASE HELP US AT ONCE (Crabb 1980:73; original emphasis).

The 1930s saw further political changes in the community. The local church was completed under the direction of Reverend Partridge, who also started compulsory education for the children and instituted the Sunday school. Continuing Churchill's decree, the resident ministers acted as commissioners and magistrates for the island, and it is during this period that we find the first attempts to restructure the Tristan community along political models of industrialised countries. William Repetto, the oldest son of Andrea, was appointed Chief Islander and Head of the Island Council in 1933.

William Repetto ("Chief Willie")

Partridge's ambitious plans were pursued by arguably the most autocratic minister Tristan da Cunha ever had, Harold Wilde, who worked on Tristan da Cunha from 1934 to 1940. Wilde served as preacher and administrator while at the same time acting as storekeeper, teacher and postmaster. Even today, the oldest members of the community have vivid memories of Wilde's 6-year reign and the iron grip he had on the community. For instance, Wilde kept a pillory to punish sinners and offenders; intercepted, read and censored all personal letters he got hold of; and supervised and rationed the distribution of food. (There is even a rumour that at one time the women had to obtain his permission to make potato cakes!) Some of his plans included the colonial expansion of the community and he ordered a group of local men to settle neighbouring Inaccessible Island. Reverend Wilde was not a popular man on Tristan, and his attitudes alienated the Tristanians more than anything else. Some of them saw no reason to worship and attend Sunday service when Wilde was on the island. Others converted to Roman Catholicism that had been brought to the island by two Irish sisters who married Tristanians and settled in 1908. Consequently, Wilde's disrespectful and patronizing behaviour was instrumental in the establishment of the Catholic Church on Tristan da Cunha in the 1930s. Today, both Anglican and Roman Catholicism are represented in the community.

Images of the 1930s

The Island Council

Traditional musicians

A catch of mackerel

The so–called "Norwegian Expedition", led by Dr Erling Christophersen, arrived in 1937 and an entire team of scientists stayed on the island for three months, examining environmental, botanical, biological and sociological aspects of Tristan da Cunha. One member of the team was Allan Crawford, who produced the first geographical survey and accurate map of the island. Crawford has had a lifelong connection with Tristan: he returned during World War II as head of the weather station, founded the first local newspaper (the *Tristan Times*), and designed the now famous "potato stamps". He also founded the Tristan da Cunha Association in England and wrote several books in which he relates his personal reminiscences of Tristan. Another member of the Norwegian Expedition was the sociologist Peter Munch. His reports indicate that the Tristan community in the late 1930s had not been affected in the least by the massive changes that had occurred in the outside world. Tristan da Cunha was not industrialised; there was no electricity, no running water supply, and no cars. (The means of transportation was oxcarts and donkeys). Munch found that only 6 out of more than 200 islanders had ever left the archipelago, and he also attested "a strong sense of cultural subordination as contrasted with the outside world". He observed that Tristanians always addressed foreigners as 'Sir', even when they were requested not to do so. For instance, when after a while Munch asked one of his Tristan friends to drop the 'Sir' and call him by the first name, the man replied: "No, Sir, we's only low and poor people" (Munch 1945:63).

Getting around on Tristan in the old days

World War II approached and the British government assessed the possibility of an open sea war in the South Atlantic Ocean, particularly after the German battle ship *Graf Spee* and German U–boats were sighted off the Tristan coast. Immediate measures were taken and the Tristan group was declared a dependency of St Helena in 1938. A local defence corps was founded (the "Tristan Defence Volunteers"), and finally the British Admiralty ordered the installation of a Naval Station on Tristan da Cunha. A naval garrison was established on the island in April 1942, run by the British Admiralty in cooperation with South African engineers and Air Force personnel. The main purpose of the station (referred to as HMS *Atlantic Isle*) was the construction of a meteorological and a wireless station.

The presence of the soldiers affected the everyday life of the Tristanians in many ways. Most of the officers brought their wives and children along, and an appointed education officer established a regular school and made the attendance of the Tristan children compulsory as well. The soldiers built living quarters with a running water supply and a sewage system, electricity, and there was even a rudimentary telephone system between the barracks. Radio contact was established with Cape Town and for the first time ever

Tristan da Cunha was in regular connection with the "outside world". The soldiers depended on the Tristanians' help, as they could not build the barracks alone. Consequently, the commanding officer employed the local men as workforce. At first he paid them with wood, paint, tobacco and food. However, when money was officially introduced as a means of payment in December 1942, the manual workers were paid two shillings a day. This was a milestone in the community's history, as it marked the end of the bartering era; from then on Tristanians could buy groceries in the local supermarket and did not depend on the (often) hazardous interception of passing ships. The community benefitted from the presence of the naval garrison in many ways. Obviously, there was a financial gain as jobs were available in construction and maintenance of the station. Moreover, the continuous presence of outsiders had socio-psychological implications as the expertise of the islanders was requested and urgently needed. The Tristanians realised for the first time that people from the outside world actually depended on their skills and labour and respected them as dedicated and meticulous workers. This resulted in the decrease of the strong sense of socio–cultural subordination that Peter Munch had diagnosed in the late 1930s.

With the end of World War II in 1945, the naval station was evacuated and all military personnel were withdrawn. However, the South African government decided to retain the meteorological station (manned with civil personnel), which meant that Tristan da Cunha continued to have permanent radio contact with the outside world and also that supply ships arrived on a regular basis. Perhaps the most far–reaching change brought by the establishment of the naval garrison was the economic transformation of island life. Reverend C P Lawrence, who served as minister on Tristan da Cunha during the war, recognised the economic potential of the island. The community, in his view, was surrounded with incredible riches at the bottom of the ocean that had hitherto not been exploited – crawfish, the local name for lobsters. There was a growing demand for lobsters in South Africa and the crawfish in Tristan waters were abundant and easy to catch. (Apparently crawfish could be caught by simply dropping a weighted pair of socks to the bottom of the sea and pulling it up shortly later – the crustaceans would persistently claw onto the wool!). Upon his return to Cape Town, Reverend Lawrence set out to devise a fishing scheme and lobbied in favour of commercial fishing. When a trial run proved promising, the Tristan Development Corporation (TDC) was formed in 1949, obtaining exclusive rights to establish a permanent fishing industry on the island. The plan was to employ virtually the entire local workforce, the men in off–shore fishing and the women in crawfish processing in the canning factory. The TDC's economic interest led to rapid changes in the local community. The traditional subsistence economy was replaced by a paid labour economy, and the traditional way of life was modified as a result of the creation of permanent jobs with regular working hours. The development scheme brought considerable benefits to the island as the TDC guaranteed full medical, social and educational amenities to the local community.

The socio–economic commitment of the TDC had political implications as well. The exclusive fishing concession of a South African company led to the presence of South African businessmen who developed private interests in the island. As a result, the British government and the office of the Commonwealth felt an urgent need to be formally represented on Tristan da Cunha. The decision was made that a resident British Administrator should be sent to the island to represent the interests of the islanders as well as those of the Commonwealth. With the arrival of Mr H P Elliott in January 1950, the first administrator directly appointed by the British government, the political structure of the island was transformed. The former system of ministers and missionaries who interferred with island life more or less at whim had finally come to an end. Mr Elliott (whose principal duty was "to act for the people of Tristan in their relations with the company") immediately reinstated the Island Council, appointing Willie Repetto as Chief Islander and ten Tristanians, as well as two company representatives, as councillors to assist him in his decisions.

In sum, the 1950s saw unprecedented changes in virtually all domains of everyday life. These changes were by nature *economic*, as the community was restructured from subsistence to paid labour economy; *political*, as the presence of the Commonwealth resulted in a reformation of the community's political structure; *social* and *socio-psychological*, as outsiders were permanently residing on Tristan da Cunha, bringing their know–how to the island while by the same time depending on the islanders' expertise (particularly in fishing); and *educational*, as British teachers were commissioned to set up a regular school system and formal education became compulsory for all local children. Tristan da Cunha in the 1950s enjoyed an economic boom and the living conditions and housing standards improved almost overnight. The changes brought about by the development scheme led to a breathtaking transformation of the traditional Tristanian way of life within a few years. Tristan was undergoing modernization and moved towards a British standard of living, and it looked as if the islanders would adapt to the outside world and complete these changes quickly. Then, however, destiny struck yet again. Nobody had anticipated what would happen in October 1961, and the community received a blow that eventually had a more long–lasting effect than any other single event before or after: the volcano erupted.

1.5 Evacuation, return and economic prosperity (1961 – 2003)

Peter Wheeler took over as administrator in 1961, and he continued the affairs of his predecessor. It was a Sunday – August 6 1961 – and the community was congregated in church, when all of a sudden the earth began trembling. Radio messages from Cape Town confirmed that the tremors had been recorded there and the administrator sent an urgent inquiry to the Foreign Office. No immediate measures were taken as British scientists were of the opinion that the volcanic activities were caused by underwater tectonic movements; they calmed the fears of the community, claiming that the tremors were not permanent and that there was no reason for concern. However, the activities intensified, big cracks appeared and disappeared in the ground, and on August 22 twenty–four tremors were recorded on a single day, resulting in cracked walls and jammed doors in the houses on the eastern side of the settlement. The heaviest tremor occurred on September 17, causing a massive rockslide near the canning factory. Administrator Peter Wheeler was in his house and described this harrowing experience as follows: "Suddenly the walls heaved, the floor trembled and for one sickening second the roof threatened to cave in" (Crabb 1980:105). However, the British government did not make any concrete evacuation plans.

Finally, on October 9 1961, the volcano erupted about two hundred metres to the east of the Settlement, and there was a slow yet constant lava flow down in the direction of the two landing beaches. Wheeler took immediate action and ordered a total evacuation to the potato patches and then to neighbouring Nightingale Island. The SOS signals were picked up by the Dutch cruise ship MS *Tjisadane* bound for Table Bay. The Tristanians could only collect their bare necessities before they were transported to Cape Town. On board the *Tjisadane* they looked at their houses again, many of them with tears in their eyes as they thought they would never return to the island. In Cape Town harbour, they were welcomed by crowds of curious South Africans who had come to see the inhabitants of the world's loneliest island. The Tristanians stayed in Cape Town for a while, and were under the impression that they would remain in South Africa for much longer. A few weeks later, however, they were told to pack their bags again and to move on to England.

They arrived in Southampton on November 3rd 1961. The British government was at a loss as to where they should be resettled and a number of plans were considered – among them resettlement in northern Scotland or on the Falkland Islands. It was finally decided that they should be housed temporarily at Pendell Camp, an unused army camp in Redhill, Surrey. The arrival in England and the resettlement in unfamiliar surroundings were traumatic for the community, particularly for the elderly. The vast majority of

Tristanians had never left the island before and were not used to the British climate and local viruses. Many of them suffered from chest infections or influenza and, within the first two months, three elderly Tristanians died of pneumonia. However, the cohesion of the community was maintained as nearly all of them stayed together, but this no doubt was little comfort considering the shock caused by the evacuation and the worries as to whether they would ever see their homes again.

A few months later they were resettled in Calshot Camp, a former Royal Air Force station near Southampton. Families could have their own houses in Calshot, and they were able to form their own little community including a chapel, community hall and post office in a nearby general store.

Charlie and Richard Green in English exile

The Southampton area had another advantage, as there was a strong demand for labour and most Tristanians found jobs in local factories and companies. These jobs facilitated their integration into the outside world. However, even though the Tristanians were treated kindly by most people, a number of things happened that made it difficult for them to embrace the idea of permanent settlement in the UK. Groceries were stolen when they were left unattended; an elderly Tristanian (who had only one arm as a result of an accident in the fishing factory) was mugged and beaten up by local "Teddy Boys"; street vendors and Jehovah's Witnesses pestered them; and a number of scientists turned up intent on studying them for a wide variety of purposes. In the words of one Tristanian: "they treated us like we was pigs". The scientific attention they received was unwelcome and some researchers upset the Tristanians tremendously. For instance, a psychologist diagnosed that most of the children were language impaired, and an ophthalmologist claimed that, within a few generations, the entire population would be blind as a result of continued in–breeding. Moreover, the "story" of the Tristanians was of great interest to newspapers, and journalists extensively covered the "clash of cultures" and the experiences of the islanders in the outside world. Not a day passed without a newspaper report, and the Tristanians received more attention than they cared for. Life in the public eye and the political discussions about their status and future alienated them considerably. They were particularly annoyed when a Member of Parliament filed a petition that Tristan da Cunha should be used as a test site for nuclear weapons as the island had been "abandoned by its inhabitants". As a consequence, the islanders, particularly the older generation, expressed a wish to return to the South Atlantic at the first possible opportunity.

A Tristanian boy experiences modern times at Calshot Camp, Southampton

In January 1962, the Royal Society sent an expedition to Tristan da Cunha with the aim of investigating the causes and effects of the eruption. The scientists reported that there was considerable lava flow but that it had missed the settlement by just 100 metres. Only one house in the settlement had been destroyed (see illustration of this overleaf).

The earthquakes had changed the drainage pattern on Tristan, but the main damage was that 25 acres of cultivated land were covered by volcanic debris. Worst of all, the two landing beaches and the canning factory were buried under 20 metres of lava. It was also discovered that some of the houses had been looted, that drawers and doors were forced open and that clothing and papers were scattered over the floor. Moreover, the safe in the post office was broken open, the sheep and most of the cattle had been butchered. It eventually turned out that some valuables that the islanders left behind in the hectic evacuation situation were stolen, presumably by sailors who had clandestinely landed on the island while the Tristanians were in England. The expedition's final report to the government concluded that even though the volcano was still glowing and very hot – 200 degrees centigrade at night – the eruption had terminated and repatriation should be considered.

The Tristanians were overjoyed when the results of the report were made public. When a vote was held, 148 voted in favour of an immediate return to the island (and only five opted to stay in England). An advance party consisting of twelve men was sent ahead to grow potatoes, repair the houses and boats, and to attend to the remaining livestock. The remaining Tristanians arrived in two parties, the first in April 1963 and the second in November of the same year. The first years were hard: the potato seed imported from England was infested with root worm and not resistant to the violent gales in the South Atlantic Ocean, and the crop failed for two years in a row. Sheep from the Falkland Islands were imported along with chickens but it took the livestock a long time to recover.

The former home of Dennis Green,
the only house destroyed by the 1961 volcano eruption

The dramatic evacuation and the two "Volcano Years" in England affected the islanders more than any other event in the history of the community. The unintended exposure to the norms of the outside world had changed the Tristanians in many ways. With the exception of the elderly generation, they adopted modern dress and entertainment. At the Saturday night dances they now danced to new tunes (such as the twist and rock 'n' roll) and the traditional dances accompanied by the old accordion tunes – such as the donkey dance and the pillow dance – quickly became outmoded and old–fashioned. There was more entertainment in the 1960s than ever before, as the islanders were introduced to bingo and card games and a cinema was set up in the main hall. They adapted to the outside world with remarkable speed in the two "Volcano Years" and the rapid adoption of a western lifestyle resulted in socio–psychological changes also. Quite rightly, the Tristanians were proud of their exceptional ability to cope with a difficult situation and the professional expertise they gained in England helped them fit back in the world they knew best. The sense of "cultural subordination" that Peter Munch had found so persistent in the late 1930s was definitely gone, replaced with healthy self–confidence and pride in their will and ability to survive as a community.

Dancing the twist and rock 'n' roll was among the many changes
which came to Tristan after the volcano years

Despite the initial hardships after the return to Tristan, the islanders' living conditions were soon to improve. Modernisation took place almost immediately: new radio telephone equipment was installed (for the first time enabling a direct contact with London!), tractors replaced the traditional ox carts, and soon after the first Land Rovers and cars were brought to the island. The crawfish industry resurfaced and a new fishing company – the South Atlantic Island Development Corporation (SAIDC) – was established in 1964; its subsidiary, the Tristan Investment (Pty), guaranteed full employment to the entire community. The SAIDC built a new on–shore factory and a new harbour, about half a mile to the west of the lava stream, and the men were employed as workforce when it was constructed. Calshot Harbour was opened on January 2nd 1967, and when the fishing factory was completed shortly after, the crawfish industry provided permanent jobs. The fishing company also provided all the households with electricity. Electric light replaced the old–style oil lamps and refrigerators and deep freezers allowed long–term food preservation.

Albert Glass back on Tristan (1964)

As a result of the renewed economic prosperity the community modernized quickly. The 1970s and 1980s saw an unprecedented economic boom and money poured in. The islanders could afford to import articles from Cape Town that were virtually unknown a few years before, such as cars and motorcycles. Electric appliances, video recorders and furniture were bought, and the steady income meant that from the mid-1980s, many Tristanians could afford to expand their houses. A new school building was completed in 1975, the supermarket was enlarged, and a wider range of foods and fashion became available. A local museum and craft centre was built, and the Tristanian received a community centre, a pub, and a café, as well as their own swimming pool. The prosperity had important implications for education as well: in the early 1980s overseas teaching programmes became available in England and on St Helena. The first Tristanian teenagers left in 1983, and today many 15–year olds are offered the opportunity to receive secondary education off the island. Similarly, adults are encouraged to undergo further job training on St Helena and more Tristanians than ever before leave the island for further education and training. This is in line with the trend to replace expatriates, who formerly were responsible for the organization of the departments, with equally qualified Tristanians trained abroad. At the time of writing, the posts of the treasurer, the postmaster, the manager of the supermarket, as well as the head positions of the Education, Agriculture and Public Works Departments are all held by Tristanians. In addition, islanders have increasingly begun to spend holidays in Cape Town in recent years.

Girls at a birthday party back on Tristan in 1964

In brief, the Tristanians today have an altogether different life style from that of their great–grandparents 100 years ago. Nowadays, the living conditions on Tristan da Cunha are comfortable, and the standards of the houses certainly resemble those in the UK. Most technological innovations, such as electronic mail, Internet access, and satellite telephone, have made an appearance on the island. The island receives the BBC World Service, and the latest asset, satellite television, became available in January 2001. As a result, Tristan da Cunha today resembles places in the outside world in many ways.

Chapter 2

Life on Tristan da Cunha today

"Physically, the island is their universe, but mentally, it isn't anymore."
David Smallman, British Governor of St Helena, January 1999

The historical account in Chapter 1 has illustrated that the community has come a long way in a very short time. The changes that have occurred since WWII are drastic indeed: the bartering era came to an end when money was introduced in 1942, the economy was remodelled from subsistence to paid labour, and the living standards improved considerably after the two "Volcano Years" in English exile. So what is it like to live on Tristan da Cunha today? To what extent have the changes affected every–day life on Tristan da Cunha? How do the Tristanians face the challenges of the 21st century, while at the same time maintaining their cultural heritage and age–old traditions?

This chapter addresses these questions and provides an overview of several aspects of life on Tristan da Cunha. We start with a general topographic and geographical description of the island and then go on to describe the settlement and community life. Finally, we present life on other parts of Tristan as well as on its neighbouring islands.

2.1 General

Technically, the Tristan da Cunha group is an archipelago as it consists of several islands: Tristan da Cunha, Nightingale, Inaccessible and Gough. Whereas the former three are grouped together, Gough Island lies 230 nautical miles (426 km) to the south. The principal and by far the biggest island of the group is Tristan da Cunha; it is also the only island with a permanent population. The climate is maritime, with a constant humid atmosphere and heavy rainfalls (the annual average is 1,676 millimetres or 65 inches). The temperature range is moderate, reaching up to 33C (91F) on a hot summer day and never falling below 2C (36F) in winter.

All the islands in the archipelago are of volcanic origin. They are situated along the Mid–Atlantic Ridge, along which we also find islands such as the Azores, St Helena, Ascension, and Iceland. These islands have different ages, and Tristan da Cunha, formed approximately one million years ago, is one of the youngest volcanic islands in the entire Atlantic Ocean. Nightingale Island, on the other hand, is one of the oldest islands; it is more than 18 million years old and heavily eroded. It is thus a curious fact that one of the oldest and one of the youngest islands in the Atlantic are only 30 kilometres apart.

Tristan da Cunha proper covers approximately 110 square kilometres; it is roughly circular in shape and some 37 km in circumference. Shaped like a symmetrical volcanic cone, it rises from the bottom of the South Atlantic Ocean to an altitude of 5,500 metres (17,900 ft), 2,048 m (6,760 ft) of which are above sea level. Almost the entire coastline consists of steep, precipitous cliffs reaching up to 600 metres (1,800 ft). Above these cliffs is a plateau, which the islanders call "the Base", that stretches for about two kilometres before it gradually turns into steep cinder slopes that lead up to the peak. From there, a number of deep and hazardous ravines, locally referred to as 'gulches', cut across the Base, radiating down to sea level. The steep cliffs make it impossible to walk around the island along the shore. There are no firths or inlets, and there is no bay that could serve as a sheltered harbour. These topographic peculiarities have posed major problems for navigating captains, causing countless casualties when ships attempted to land at the island.

The coastline is almost entirely marked by sea cliffs. There are only two small coastal strips, one on the southern tip and one along the north–western coast of the island. The latter strip is bigger – about 30–60 metres above sea level, six kilometres long and up to one kilometre wide. This plain hosts the only village on Tristan da Cunha as well as the islanders' gardens and fields, situated about two kilometres to the south–west. The Tristanians grow mainly potatoes here, but probably most vegetables would thrive on Tristan if it were not for the occasionally tempestuous gales.

2.2 Life in the Settlement

Despite the fact that the area of the island is more than 100 square kilometres, there is only one permanently inhabited village. Its official name is *Edinburgh of the Seven Seas*, named in honour of His Royal Highness Prince Alfred, Duke of Edinburgh, who visited the island in 1867. However, the official name is rarely used; the Tristanians are quite happy to refer to it simply as 'the Settlement'.

The Settlement, as seen from the top of the volcano which erupted in 1961

About 300 people are living on Tristan today. Most of them are native Tristanians but there is also a small number of "station fellas", i.e. outsiders who reside on the island temporarily (for instance, the administrator and doctor with their families, the manager of the fishing factory, or visitors and travellers who visit the island for longer periods of time). The term "station fella" has its origins in the garrison sent to the island in WWII; the soldiers referred to their living quarters and army buildings as 'the station', and the Tristanians referred to the army personnel as 'the fellas what stop in the station', or shorter, the 'station fellas'. At the time of writing, there are 285 Tristanians, aged between a few months and 96 years. The seven family names on Tristan reflect the international atmosphere of the founding period as well as the strong nautical tradition of the colony. The present community consists of the following families, reflecting founding fathers from five different countries: the Glasses (the descendants of William Glass, the Scottish founder of the colony), the Swains (Thomas Swain, from Hastings, England), the Rogers and Hagans (Thomas Rogers and Captain Andrew Hagan, the American whalers), the Greens (Peter William Green, from Katwijk, Holland), and finally the Repettos and Lavarellos (Andrea Repetto and Gaetano Lavarello, the two Italians who settled in 1892). Some founders of the colony did not leave their names (most notably Maria Leenders and the women from St Helena) whereas others vanished without a trace – the Rileys and Møllers left in 1857, and Betty Cotton, the last descendant of Alexander Cotton, passed away in the late 1920s.

There are about 100 houses on the island. The architecture is carefully designed and adapted to life near the "Roaring Forties". From the outside the houses still bear a striking resemblance to the original cottages built by Samuel Burnell, John Nankivel and William Glass (as seen in Earle's sketch of Glass's cottage in Chapter 1). With very few exceptions they are flat, consisting of a single story and a small loft. Every house has an adjacent shed where potatoes, vegetables and tools are stored. Perhaps the main characteristic of Tristanian architecture is that all the buildings face the same direction, looking northwards to the open sea. The "scenic" aspect is not the main motivation for the uniformity of the houses, however. The views on the sea and the seemingly endless horizons are breathtaking, but the purpose of this building style is strictly functional. The colonizers realized quickly that the most forceful winds came from the northeast; by building their homes this way, the exposure to the gales was minimized. This building style has been handed down the generations ever since. In recent years the houses' exteriors have undergone some modifications and the traditional look of the village has changed somewhat. For instance, all the houses in the Settlement once had thatched roofs. However, the Tristanians have recently replaced them with corrugated steel sheets and asbestos-cement sheeting, and the last thatched roof disappeared in 1994. Another characteristic of the settlement is the hedges of New Zealand flax that are interspersed in and around the village to protect the houses and gardens from the high winds. While the outside appearance of the houses has hardly changed since the 1820s, there is very little in the interior that would resemble the old times. Most houses have a living and/or dining room facing the sea, and the bedrooms and bathroom are usually at the back, towards the towering mountain cliff. Modernization has taken place and standard appliances are found in most households; today, there are refrigerators (locally termed 'coolers'), microwave ovens, and deep freezers in almost every house. The economic boom of the 1970s and 1980s allowed many families to extend their houses and add extra rooms, and many houses now have several bedrooms.

The lay-out of the settlement resembles places in the outside world in several ways. The community has a supermarket, a post office, two churches (Saint Mary for the Anglican congregation and Saint Joseph for the Catholic community), a school and a hospital. Notwithstanding the geographical remoteness, the medical treatment of the population is guaranteed; a resident doctor (usually from South Africa) is stationed on the island to take care of minor injuries and illnesses. The local hospital is well equipped with a delivery and emergency room. The surgery room, however, is not fully operational at the moment; it was situated in the part of the building that was destroyed by the 2001 hurricane. Patients in need of surgery or special medical treatment have to go to Cape Town.

The social centre of the island is the Prince Philip Hall, located right in the heart of the village. Tristan's only pub is here; it is open nightly and the Tristanians meet for a beer, pool and darts. The adjacent hall has many uses: it is used for the Saturday night dances, bigger parties and also as a gym and for indoor sports.

The world's most remote pub

The island also has a well–stocked public library and plans are currently being developed for an adult education centre, which might house a publicly accessible computer facility. There is an open–air swimming pool, as well as a café that opens every afternoon. The island also has its own 9–hole golf course (which, however, has to be shared with grazing cows who at times do not take kindly to the low–flying golf balls).

The Café and the island's pub
(The building adjoining the pub is the Prince Philip Hall
which has been without a roof since the 2001 hurricane)

All this resembles places of the same size in Great Britain, and the settlement in many ways is as modern and "real" as villages in rural England. However, there are a number of characteristics that set Tristan apart from comparable places in the outside world. Tristan has a bank but no ATM machines. The Tristanians can only shop during the week because the supermarket is not open on Saturdays and Sundays. There is a road but no traffic lights; there are not even road signals. Then again, they would not be of much use. There is only one major road on the island, and it is only about six kilometres long. Moreover, there are no hotels, restaurants, bed and breakfasts, cinemas or theatres at all.

For the occasion of an island wedding, the Administrator's Land Rover
is nicely decorated and put at the disposition of the married couple

The social life on Tristan takes place in the Albatross Inn, the island's only (and quite possibly the world's remotest) pub, the Café, and also in the homes of the Tristanians themselves. Geophysical remoteness does not equal loneliness, and visits and get-togethers have always been an important part in the islanders' everyday lives. The Tristanians visit each other regularly, to deliver some produce, just for a chat and to exchange some news, or also to celebrate a birthday or a christening. The most grandiose and long-lasting get-together is an island wedding, where the local hall is decorated and the entire population is invited to join the party and dance. A wedding celebration may last up to 5 days.

At a major event, such as a wedding, the whole population
is invited to a dance in the community centre or in the school hall.

33

Other good reasons to celebrate are anniversaries, special holidays (such as Her Majesty's Birthday) or individual birthdays. Tristan parties are always a community effort; everybody does their share and contributes food or drinks to make sure that nobody is overwhelmed by the organisation. As the Tristan community is extraordinarily tight–knit, everybody helps each other wherever needed, and it is not uncommon to take a day off work just to help a neighbour or friend prepare a party. Women get together and bake cakes and organize food, while men arrange the facility and bring drinks.

Whereas parties and social events have always been part of the community – Augustus Earle mentioned the frequent gatherings as early as 1824 – other aspects of island life had changed considerably by the second half of the 20th century. For instance, the economic situation has undergone massive changes within the last three generations. Today, work on Tristan da Cunha is a careful and clever compromise between a modern paid labour system and the local subsistence economy. The Tristanians are hard–working people and the island continues to be virtually self–supporting. Indeed, they are proud of the fact that they produce most of their daily needs without outside help, and it is noteworthy that the community only relies on overseas funding to finance some large–capital projects, such as the acquisition of a new patrol boat or hospital equipment. The development scheme that was set out for Tristan was truly ingenious, as it managed to integrate the traditional life into a modern economical system. It was specially devised for the unique circumstances of the community and has been so successful that, to many people from the outside world, the social conditions on Tristan seem ideal. A percentage of the income from the crawfish industry, the sale of stamps, and interests from a non–local reserve fund provide the revenues to finance government activities. The income is put to good use and all the Tristanians, regardless of salary, age and sex, benefit equally. For instance, the provision of health care and education are free for the entire community, and most island families pay only a few pounds income tax a year.

Tristan's only harbour, Calshot Harbour. This was opened on 1967
and named after the Tristanians' place of residence during the "Volcano Years"

The Government is the chief employer on the island with a work force of 143, divided into 11 separate departments. The fishing industry is operated under the terms of an exclusive concession that is granted by the island. A South African company provides permanent employment for 23 and part–time employment for an additional 110 people during the fishing season. The crawfish tails, sought–after delicacies in the United States and Japan, are prepared and deep–frozen on board the ships and in the local factory, and then transported to Cape Town. The crawfish industry has had a profound impact on the ecological development of the island as well. The government and company take great care to maintain and protect the crawfish stocks around Tristan, and strict laws have been introduced. The most important regulation is that the total annual catch must not surpass 340 tons per fishing season. Commercial fishing starts in early September and lasts until the total amount is reached (which depends on the weather conditions). The fishing season ends when the annual quota is caught, and for the rest of the year the islanders continue fishing for their own private purposes.

Fishing is not just an economic activity but also a popular pastime for Tristanians of all ages

The adaptation to, and integration of, a modernized economy has led to the fact that today most Tristanians have more than one job. They are official employees of the Government and have regular working hours in their departments. During the fishing season, however, the work scheme changes and they are employed in the crawfish industry while at the same time continuing their regular jobs. (With the exception of fishermen and employees of the fishing factory, Tristanians basically work for their departments during the day and for the fishing company at night, even though working hours are more flexible.) As if that was not enough, the Tristanians at all times need to sustain their own households and constantly attend to their cattle and crops. They spend their Saturdays in the fields, growing and harvesting vegetables, and on the mountain, looking for firewood, checking on their livestock, or fishing for their personal needs.

During the September lambing season, young
lambs are caught and marked by their owners

The political structure of the community has undergone an equally successful transformation. Formerly the island had a *primus inter pares* system; Tristan was unofficially represented by a spokesman who conducted business with passing ships and acted on behalf of the entire community. The first of these representatives was William Glass, and the custom was continued by Alexander Cotton, Peter Green, and Andrea Repetto. The last representative of this honourable tradition was William Repetto, who was the last Chief Islander for life and a natural leading figure. The personality and authority of "Chief Willie", as he was respectfully called, became most evident during the difficult volcano years in English exile. He led and spoke on behalf of the Tristanians in this difficult time, and defended the community's interests when negotiating with the British government. In hindsight, it was mostly thanks to his persistence and negotiation skills that a return to the South Atlantic eventually became possible.

When Chief Willie passed away in the late 1970s, the traditional system was transformed and a democratic electoral system was introduced. Today, the government consists of a resident administrator, who is directly appointed by the Foreign Office. The administrator must act in accordance with advice from the Island Council, which is composed of eight members who are elected by the community and three members appointed by the administrator. A general election is held every three years and at least one member of the council must be a woman. (At the time of writing, five women are members of the Island Council). Tristanians willing to be nominated as Chief Islander are candidates for the post, and if there is more than one candidate then the person who receives the greatest number of votes in the election is declared 'Chief Islander'.

In their spare time, the Tristanians have a number of hobbies. VCRs were introduced to the island in the early 1980s; most families have substantial video collections that they share with other community members. Satellite television became available in January 2001, enabling them for the first time to watch live TV in their homes. However, at least for the moment, they only have one channel. Two traditional pastimes that have been handed down through the generations are knitting and the manufacturing of model long boats (the traditional sailing boats of Tristan, see below). Even though they have recently started to import wool from South Africa, the Tristanians produce their own island wool. The sheep are sheared once a year and the women get together in their traditional "carding gangs", sharing the strenuous work of washing, picking, spinning and carding the wool (much to the dismay of the men who flee the houses taken over by the carding gangs and keep themselves busy elsewhere). Some Tristanian women even knit as they walk out to their potato patches, and they knit everything from pullovers, hats, scarves, and socks to cute little toy penguins.

The men have their own traditional hobbies as well and many of them build model boats. The longboats have always symbolized island life and are used for the traditional sailing trips to neighbouring Nightingale Island (see below). The models are about 40 to 50 centimetres long; they have a canvas keel, a mast and two sails and are painted in the boat's original colours. Tristanian handicrafts are on display in the island's craft centre and tourists buy them for a truly unique souvenir of Tristan da Cunha.

The Tristanians spend a substantial amount of their free time in the kitchen; they always bake their own bread and fast food is unknown to them. Consequently, then, Tristanian cuisine is another area of everyday life where old mixes with new. Traditional Tristan dishes include roast mutton, stuffed with mashed potatoes, or the 'Tristan pudding' (consisting of mashed potatoes, sugar, flour and eggs, which are mixed and boiled in a cloth bag) but new recipes have been added after more exotic spices became available in the 1960s. One all-time favourite has survived the competition with deep-frozen goods, curries and all kinds of imported sauces and marinades, and that is the "Tristan taters". The predilection for home-grown potatoes has never changed and probably never will. Potatoes, grown in the patches, about two miles south-west of the settlement, have always been the islanders' main diet, and the Tristanians have developed an extraordinarily wide variety of potato-based recipes for all seasons. (See the Tristan recipes at the end of this chapter.)

2.3 Life outside the Settlement

The Settlement is situated on a plateau along Tristan's north-western coast. The only road on the island spans almost the entire plain. It is about six kilometres long and connects the settlement with The Bluff, a steep cliff at the other end of the flat level. Immediately behind the Settlement, the road winds its way towards the Hillpiece, through what the Tristanians call *The Walley* (i.e. 'valley'; see Chapter 3 for a description of the local dialect), and then downhill to the potato patches. The patches are of utmost economic importance to the community and generations of uncertainty and hardship have made the Tristanians true experts in the cultivation of potatoes. They have developed their own techniques to maximize the crops (such as the usage of wool, guano, decomposed crawfish shells – or, in the olden days, sea kelp – as fertilizer). Each family has their own planting method and everybody takes great pride in their gardens and crops, especially in November when the patches are in full bloom. All in all, there are more than 500 potato patches on the plateau; all of them are nicely fenced off with walls built out of volcanic rock. The plots of brown soil contrast with the green grass of the plateau, and from the top of the mountain the neat arrangement of square patches resembles a giant chessboard.

Tending to the patches is almost a year-round activity. The season starts with spading in July; the fields are dug up and made arable, and all the weeds are pulled off and removed. In September and October, the seeds are planted and just before Christmas the first "taters" are harvested. The digging season lasts several months and the last crops are dug out in late March or even early April. The potatoes are extremely important to the community and it is more than likely that, without the potato patches, Tristan da Cunha would not be inhabited today. In the days of William Glass, Peter Green, and Chief Willie Repetto, the production of potatoes guaranteed self-sufficiency and independence from the anything but reliable trade opportunities with passing ships.

The potato patches and camping huts, southwest of the Settlement, as seen from the Hillpiece

Even today, when most Tristanians could probably afford to import vegetables from South Africa, potato growing continues to be one of the activities that unites the community. The patches are much more than simply the securing of a main diet; they represent a significant part of the islanders' social life. Families, relatives, neighbours and friends go out to the fields together, helping each other out wherever assistance is needed. Men and women co–operate in the digging, sorting out and packing of the "taters", and when the hard work is done they meet at one of the houses for refreshments and a chat. The potatoes clearly symbolize the community's independence and will to sustain themselves, and independence is the last thing the Tristanians would want to lose.

A Tristanian family planting "taters", the islanders' main diet

The cultivation of the plateau secures provisions and food for the community and the environment is used in numerous ways. Tristanians are keen farmers, and every family has their own livestock, consisting of cattle, sheep and poultry. However, grazing land is precious and the preservation of the islands' natural resources is vital. The Island Council has set down a set of strict laws to regulate the breeding of cattle and sheep on the settlement plain. To ensure that the limited pastures are not overexploited and that the grazing land is not in danger of erosion, families are only allowed to keep a maximum of two cows and seven sheep. To some outsiders, the limitation of private property may sound like an intrusion into the individuals' lives, but the Tristanians have long ago realized that the community's survival depends on the cooperation and *de jure* equality of all its members.

Everyday life on Tristan mainly takes place in and around the Settlement, but other places of the island are frequented also. Of particular importance is a smaller plateau on the south–western tip of the island – The Caves and Stony Hill. It is very hazardous to walk from the settlement to the Caves along the beach; the beach line is interrupted by steep rugged cliffs that rise up to 150 metres, and rock falls or unpredictably high waves pose a constant danger. Consequently, the only way to get to the southern plain is either a hike over the mountain or to travel by boat. The Caves and Stony Hill are thus not easily accessible and not permanently inhabited. However, the Tristanians have camping huts and go to the Caves several times a year, sometimes just for a couple of days off but usually to attend to the cattle. Grazing land is limited on the settlement plain, and the islanders keep about 200 head of cattle at the Caves. The cattle are wild as they are left to themselves. It is a real experience to watch the bullocks stampede across the plain and quite an adventure to catch them!

The area known as the Caves and Stonyhill Plain on the southwestern tip of the island
(The caves themselves are only visible from the sea)

One of the highlights in the annual routine of the Tristanians is the so–called "Round the Beaches" tour in October. The first stop is The Caves, about half way around the island. Here the new–born calves are caught and marked, and the huts are checked and repaired. Then the Tristanians go around the island to Sandy Point at the eastern tip of the island, where a few bullocks are kept also. It takes the men several days to go "Round the Beaches"; it is a great social experience after the long, dark and somewhat uneventful winter months and facing the wild cattle is always an exciting challenge.

Sandy Point, at the easternmost extremity of the island, is a most unusual place. Tristan has its own vegetation which is adapted to the stormy gales. The highest vegetation types on Tristan are ferns and the so–called "Island Trees" (*Phylica arborea*), which grow up to two metres tall. Sandy Point, however, differs from the rest of the island as it is well protected from the north–western winds. The Tristanians keep apple orchards and plum trees here and produce large quantities of fruit, as the climate is mild.

Moreover, there are also massive pine trees, up to 50 metres tall. They were planted in the 1950s as part of a lumber development scheme that later failed. The huge, dark pines contrast with the rest of the island, and the apples that grow here are delicious. Until a couple of years ago the community used to have traditional "Appling Days" where everybody, both old and young, took a day off to row to Sandy Point and to harvest apples. The Appling Days (or *Happling Days*, as the Tristanians say) were a great way to combine work and fun, and the entire community enjoyed a day out. However, this tradition has been somewhat abandoned since the 1980s; today only a handful of people go out to pick the apples for the rest of the community.

A traditional community activity that has survived is the so–called "Ratting Day". Until quite recently rats were a major problem on the island. In 1882, the *HB Paul* was shipwrecked at Sandy Point, but the Captain and crew survived and made their way to the Settlement. The Captain knew that the ship was infested with vermin but did not dare to inform the islanders, as he feared that they would set the ship on fire and burn the cargo. It did not take the rats long to get ashore. They had no natural enemies and virtually overran the island. The rats caused great damage to island life, particularly as they decimated the bird colonies and destroyed plants and crops. The islanders became aware of the imminent danger and organized special days where all the members of the community would go out to exterminate vermin: the so–called "Ratting Days". Even though modern technology has decimated the rat population considerably, this old tradition continues to the present day. Every year in May or June, the entire workforce is given a day off to hunt rats from dawn till dusk. It is usually the men who go after rats with their dogs, while the women cook meals and provide beverages and snacks. The Ratting Days are a real community event and the Tristanians celebrate the evening with a traditional get–together and a communal dance in the Prince Philip Hall. There are also prizes for the gangs that catch the most rats, and there is even a special prize for the longest rat–tail! Another favourite tradition is the so-called *Okalolies* on New Year's Eve, when the men dress up and wander around the settlement with masks (or, in former times, with painted faces) to scare the folks. The origin of the term *Okalolies* is not clear; it is quite plausible that it represents an anglicized form of the Afrikaans words *Olie Kolonies*, best translated as 'old ugly men'. Interestingly, the Malay community in Cape Town has a similar custom; on New Year's Eve, they dress up in exotic costumes and go from house to house to visit people, playing instruments such as the banjo. This suggests that the Tristan *Okalolies* have their origins in this Cape Malay custom, and that it was introduced to Tristan by Maria Glass, who, as a Cape Creole, may indeed have been a member of the Malay community.

In brief, then, most of the community life takes place in and around the settlement. However, activities are not confined to the settlement plain and the Tristanians occasionally visit other beaches around the island as well. The part of the island they visit less frequently is the mountain, i.e. the slopes along the ridge of the volcanic crater. The topographical set–up of the island is best described as a huge step, as a massive wall of black basalt cliffs, up to 700 metres high, separates the lower coastal plains from the flatter mountain level. Above these cliffs is a plateau, called 'the Base', stretching for about two kms before steep cinder slopes lead up to the peak. Deep and hazardous ravines, the "gulches", intersect the Base, going all the way down to the shoreline.

A view of the Base, showing fern bushes and "island trees"

The vegetation on the mountain is strikingly different from the flora on the coast below. The type of vegetation here is characterized by fern bushes interspersed with "island trees". Even though not very high, the undergrowth is very thick in some places and this makes transportation difficult. Moreover, the high humidity and frequent rainfalls on Tristan result in bogs and swamps, and the unreliability of the ground makes the Base even more treacherous.

The islanders keep wild sheep on the Base, and there are no rules as to how many sheep can be kept on the mountain. The relative inaccessibility of the mountain impedes the control of sheep breeding. Consequently, then, the Tristanians only go up to the Base in order to catch sheep, to fetch firewood, fix up fences, or to walk to more remote places of the island, avoiding the dangerous beach walks. Climbing and descending from the Base is hazardous and definitely not recommended for people afraid of heights. Good nerves are required when you are climbing down a rocky path with a sheep on your back and you are one foot away from a 100–metre precipice.

The peak of the volcano, as seen from The Base

41

The least frequented area of the island provides the most breath–taking views: the top of the volcanic peak. Tristanians have no real reason to climb all the way up to the peak (which is more than 2,060 metres high), and very few of them go up regularly. In fact, most of the Tristanians born after the volcano years have never been there. The trip from the Settlement to the crater inside the volcano peak is strenuous and takes anything between three to six hours. The hike is a unique and unforgettable adventure. It passes through five different climate zones and offers the most spectacular views of Tristan and the seemingly endless horizons of the South Atlantic Ocean. Standing on top of the world's loneliest island, watching the deep blue of the ocean all around, is an experience hikers cherish for all time.

The top of the island. The crater inside the volcano peak,
with Inaccessible Island just visible in the background

The steep cliffs hide the coastal plains completely, and the settlement and potato patches cannot be seen from the peak. However, the views of the entire Base and the gulches radiating in all directions are spectacular. The neighbouring islands, Nightingale and Inaccessible, 35 kilometres away, look so close that they appear to be almost within swimming distance of Tristan.

2.4 Life off the island

Tristan da Cunha is the only island in the archipelago which has a permanent population. The Tristanians never had the intention of colonizing the surrounding islands, but they soon began to visit and explore them. The first recorded trip to Inaccessible Island dates from 1821, just five years after the start of settlement on Tristan, when William Glass and his companions saved the survivors of the wrecked *Blendon Hall* (see Chapter 1).

Through most of the 19th century the Tristanians ventured out in smaller rowing boats or lifeboats that were given to them as presents. However, travelling to Nightingale and Inaccessible was considerably facilitated by a new kind of sailing boat, the so–called "longboat", which was brought to Tristan by Andrea Repetto and Gaetano Lavarello, the two Italian sailors who arrived in 1892. Repetto and Lavarello had considerable knowledge in this metier as they taught the craftsmanship of building big sailing boats to the people on Tristan. There was no lumber on the island in the late 19th century, and the Tristanians originally built their sailing boats of driftwood. They covered the frames with canvas or old mailbags and made them waterproof with oil and paint. The islanders learnt the boatbuilding trade quickly and developed considerable skills: they have lost only two boats in more than one hundred years of sailing to neighbouring islands. Long ago, while sailing to Nightingale, one boat leaked and burst, but luckily there were no casualties and the crew was picked up by a longboat following behind. The second boating loss was the *Canton*, which was lost just off Nightingale's Landing Rock in April 2002.

Two Tristan longboats off the Settlement

A more modern technique, namely the usage of fibreglass, was introduced only in the 1980s. However, improved technology has not changed the traditional look of the boats; when the sails are up, the boats still look as if they came straight from the late 19th century.

Sydney Glass relaxing with his pipe in a longboat

In recent years, the use of longboats has decreased somewhat. Formerly the longboats were the only means of transport to less accessible parts of Tristan or to the neighbouring islands. Today, however, outboard motors have come to the island and engine–driven barges, RIBs (Rigid Inflatable Boats) and powerboats are predominantly used. The community also possesses a high–tech patrol boat that allows the fishery officers to check the island and to catch boats poaching in Tristan waters. Today, the longboats are only used for the traditional sailing trips to Nightingale Island and are stored away for most of the year.

Going to Nightingale is a highlight in the annual routine of the islanders. Each of the eight boats has its own crew, and the sailing trips are races between the different crews and their respective coxswains. The 32–kilometre trip takes between three and six hours, depending on the wind and waves. The crew of the fastest sailing boat over a one-year period receives a trophy, which has to be defended the following year. The weather in the South Atlantic is unpredictable and the voyages always carry a potential hazard. The wind can turn at amazing speed, and there is no need to describe just how dangerous weather changes are for sailing boats travelling to a particular destination. More than once trips had to be interrupted when the wind turned or dropped; sometimes the landing conditions on Nightingale were not suitable and the crews had to sleep on the open sea. The worst incident occurred in 1958, when fog suddenly descended and the wind direction changed by 180 degrees within a few minutes. Two boats drifted out to sea and the crews had to suffer for more than five days before they were finally rescued.

A Tristan longboat sets sail off the landing rock at Nightingale Island

As for the other islands in the archipelago, the one Tristanians visit most often is Nightingale. In many ways Nightingale resembles Tristan da Cunha as it was before modernization began. Virtually the entire island is covered with two–metre high tussock grass, and the paths need constant attention or else they grow over in a few months. The islanders have living and cooking shacks on the eastern coast of the island, and store their boats on a cliff by the landing rock. The years of uncertainty and dependency on bartering with passing ships have made the Tristanians independent and inventive. In the olden days, bird fat was used as oil for the lamps and they even produced their own matches with sulphuric acid and wood splinters! These survival skills become most obvious on Nightingale, as it is here that the Tristanians depend most on their natural resources. There is no electricity and no running water supply on the island; drinking water has to be brought along from Tristan, as the bird colonies have polluted the island's few brooks.

The shacks which the islanders have on Nightingale Island are small yet comfortable, and the cooking shacks have open fireplaces. Before World War II, they would sleep in a cave near the landing rock, where they cut holes in the ground to be used as cooking and sleeping places. Then the first living and cooking shacks were built in the late 1940s. Several Tristanians share a shack and are jointly responsible for maintenance and renovation. The shacks, some 8-20 metres above sea level, are built of wood or concrete, with doors and windows, and asbestos-cement sheets as roofs, with a size of up to 20 square metres. The Tristanians take good care of their shacks even though they spend only a few weeks each year there. This is also for the reason that Nightingale represents a traditional get-away and change from the every-day life on Tristan.

Shacks on Nightingale Island[1]

---

[1] All the shacks shown in this photo were destroyed by the 2001 hurricane. Only a handful of shacks survived winds of up to 140 kilometres an hour and waves up to ten metres high (see the Epilogue). The Tristanians are currently rebuilding them, but since they have their priorities in reparing the damage caused on Tristan, it may take quite a while until Nightingale returns to normality as well.

The Tristanians predominantly go to Nightingale to collect penguin eggs (on the so-called "egg trip") or guano for fertilizer in the patches, and the huge colonies of petrels, shearwaters and penguins provide large quantities of it. The work takes about two to three days and then the wait begins for the south–eastern winds to enable them to sail back to Tristan. Patience is needed though, and on one occasion the Tristanians had to wait for a whole month before they could set sail and return to Tristan again.

Rockhopper penguins on Nightingale

The wildlife of Nightingale Island is superb. The bird life is rich and varied; the Tristan archipelago is the biggest breeding site for albatrosses and petrels in the South Atlantic Ocean. Whereas the human population has had a considerable impact on the bird stocks of Tristan, a huge variety has survived on the neighbouring islands that are visited rather infrequently. The almost impenetrable tussock grass protects the nests from scavengers, and Nightingale hosts large colonies of yellow nose albatross, great shearwater, buntings, and the unique flightless rail. Tens of thousands of rockhopper penguins have established rookeries and it is quite an amazing sight when they all leave the island at the same time in order to migrate to more southern areas. Countless groups of rock-hopper penguins leave their habitat and hop somewhat clumsily downhill, right through the islanders' shacks, to get to the ocean. There they line up in long queues at the best places and jump into the water, one after another, to begin their long journey to the breeding grounds on the Kerguelen Islands in the southern Indian Ocean.

Nest of a yellow-nosed albatross on Nightingale Island

Two Tristan boys holding up young yellow-nosed albatrosses ("Mollies")

The maritime life is unique as well. The seas around the islands of Tristan are rich in fish as well as lobster and octopus. A large variety of fish species are found, such as the (perhaps endemic) fivefinger, snoek, bluefish, stumpnose, steenbrass, soldier, mackerel, and several types of sharks. Fur seals, elephant seals, and sea lions can constantly be seen on the cliffs and rocks of Nightingale Island, and the rare Shepherd's Beaked Whale and the Southern Right Whale also visit the area.

Inaccessible Island seen from Tristan da Cunha

About eight kilometres to the north is the third and much less visited island of the archipelago, Inaccessible Island. Its topography is strikingly different. Black cliffs rise steeply out of the ocean, and from afar Inaccessible looks like a dark fortress (or like a rhinoceros lying on its stomach, with its horn pointing up). Indeed, even from close range first–time visitors can hardly imagine where landing is possible. Inaccessible is visited even less frequently than neighbouring Nightingale, and Tristanians mostly go to the island to collect apples on Salt Beach.

Inaccessible Island viewed from Nightingale Island

Landing at this island is difficult, but this did not prevent people from attempting to colonize it. Inaccessible was the site of the famous wreck of the *Blendon Hall* in 1821, and the 50 survivors of the disaster stayed on the island for almost two months until William Glass and his companions came to their rescue. After the involuntary stay of the castaways from the *Blendon Hall*, there were at least two projects for a permanent settlement. The Stoltenhoff brothers from Germany were the first would-be colonizers; they arrived in 1871 and intended to settle on the island for good. Their plan was similar to the development scheme developed by Jonathan Lambert early in the 19th century; they planned to exploit the natural resources of the island and to sell agricultural products and meat to passing ships. However, the plans of the Stoltenhoffs were short–lived and they were forced to leave the island after two years.

Another colonization plan was developed by Reverend Harold Wilde, who served as minister in the late 1930s. He feared that Tristan might become overpopulated and that the natural resources of the main island would be unable to sustain the community. Consequently, he ordered several men to sail to Inaccessible and to build huts and cultivate fields. However, there was neither success nor enthusiasm for the project and the Tristanians immediately abandoned the project after Wilde left in 1940.

Today, the Tristanians rarely go to Inaccessible, the reason being that the island is now legally protected as a natural habitat. The Island Council recognized the vital importance of the island in preserving natural resources and officially declared it a natural reserve in March 1994. The island is of global importance as it has numerous endemic species, most notably the world's smallest flightless bird, the Inaccessible Island rail, or "island cock" as the Tristanians would say. It is also significant as a breeding site for at least 16 seabird species, including the northernmost population of the wandering albatross. Tristan islanders retain the right to collect apples, driftwood and guano, but access for other purposes is limited and all living resources are strictly protected.

The most distant island of the archipelago is Gough Island, more than 400 kilometres to the south. Gough is not inhabited but has a South African meteorological station that is permanently manned. Apart from the station there are no traces of civilization at all. Literally speaking, the island belongs to the birds; hundreds of thousands of birds have their breeding and nesting grounds here, and it is here where they start migrating to other areas in or around the Atlantic, flying as far north as Newfoundland. Humans rarely leave the station and dare to go hiking on the hills only infrequently. (Like all the other islands, Gough is very hazardous. Since the 1960s at least three meteorologists have been taken by surprise by sudden changes in the weather, lost their orientation, and perished).

A special wildlife management plan has been devised to protect the unique environmental status of Gough Island. The UNESCO declared Gough Island a World Heritage Site and the island is now completely protected. The people of Tristan are keenly aware of the need to live in harmony with their natural environment. The status of Gough Island and Inaccessible as official nature reserves means that some 44% of the land area in the Tristan archipelago is under protection and set aside for conservation, which may well merit another entry in the Guinness Book of Records.

Conrad Glass, the island's only policeman

Tristan Recipes

The Tristanians have developed a wide range of potato-based recipes. This is due to the local climate, in which potatoes thrive, and to the limited supplies of food and provisions in earlier times. On occasion, no ship would call for three years, so the Tristanians had to use whatever they could produce locally, traditionally potatoes and fish.

Crawfish Hash

10   medium potatoes
2   large rock lobsters (crawfish)
2   large onions
2   tablespoons of cooking oil
1   tablespoon of butter or margarine
1/2 cup of milk

Peel and wash the potatoes, then bring them to the boil in a saucepan. Wash and remove the shells of the crawfish, chop up the meat, and bring to the boil in another saucepan. After 20–25 minutes, both crawfish and potatoes should be well cooked. Peel and chop onions, mix with the cooked crawfish, and brown the mixture in the cooking oil, until the onions are tender. Mash the cooked potatoes with the milk and butter. Add the crawfish and onions to the mashed potatoes, and add salt and pepper to season.

Stuffed Roast Mutton

1   hind leg of a lamb

Stuffing:

8   medium potatoes
1   large onion
8   pieces parsley
salt and pepper to season

Cut the leg of lamb down to the first two ribs of the flank. Debone leg and remove the two ribs. When deboned, fold flap over the leg. Stitch openings of meat forming a pocket, leaving an opening for the stuffing.
    Wash and peel the potatoes and bring to the boil; mash them when they are cooked. Chop onions and parsley together and add to the mashed potatoes, salt and pepper to season. Then put the stuffing mixture into the mutton pocket. Stuff the mixture in tightly and sew up with twine or strong string. Put into the preheated oven (200C) and roast for two and a half to three hours until well done and crispy. Serve with roast potatoes and roast vegetables.

Tater Cakes

1   pound of cooked and mashed potatoes
5   ounces of flour
1   pinch of salt

(This recipe makes about 15 cakes)

Mix ingredients together until smooth. Roll out potato mixture until 1/2 inch thick. Cut potato cakes with a suitable cutter. Gather left-overs, mix, re-roll and cut, until all mixture is used. Deep-fry in cooking oil, until they are golden brown.
    Tristan tater cakes are served with sweetened cream or jam.

Fried Apple Turnovers

1   pound of cooked and mashed potatoes
5   ounces of flour
1   pinch of salt
      Stewed apples with sugar and mixed spice to taste (Jam can also be used)

Combine potato mixture and roll out until 1/4 inch thick. Cut with a saucer (or use a knife to cut around the saucer). On each round level place a level tablespoon of apple or jam. Fold over in half, prick top with a fork, and then seal and fry or deep-fry.

Spotty Dick Pudding

6   large potatoes
2   cups of flour
1   packet of seedless raisins
1   pinch of salt

Boil and mash the potatoes. Add the two cups of flour, raisins and salt. Knead the mixture until firm and form into ball shape. Put the pudding into the pudding bag, tie tightly with a strong piece of string, and boil in a saucepan for two to two and a half hours until golden brown. Serve pudding with cream, jam or butter and sugar.

Chapter 3

The language of Tristan da Cunha

*We got this slang on Tristan, the "Tristan Slang" we call it. It's not really
number one English, but it's British* (Harold Green, Tristan da Cunha, April 1999).

The geographical location of Tristan da Cunha had an effect on all areas of social life of the
community. Since language is an important part of all human behaviour and since the
island is so remote, it is not a surprise to find that the islanders have developed their own
distinctive dialect. Indeed, the local dialect, which some Tristanians refer to as "Tristan
Slang", is a unique form of colonial English and much commented on by outsiders and
expatriates; it is not found anywhere else in the English–speaking world. This last chapter
of our book discusses questions such as what Tristan da Cunha English is like, where it
came from, how it is affected by recent changes in the community, and whether isolated
communities like Tristan da Cunha participate in language change or not.

3.1 Language in isolation

Most people assume that isolated communities do not take part in language change as
mainstream communities do, and that they continue to speak more or less exactly like
their ancestors did. In this view, language simply stops changing and isolated dialects
preserve earlier forms of a language. Just such a view is expressed by a Danish journalist
who claimed that the Tristanians speak early 19th century Cockney English: "they speak
an English which went out of fashion in London's docklands in the first years of Queen
Victoria's reign" (Falk-Rønne 1967:21). The same idea is expressed in a leaflet distributed
on the RMS *St Helena*, a cruise liner that travels from Cape Town to Tristan da Cunha each
January. In a brochure distributed on the ship, travellers learn:

> Through the islanders' veins flows the blood of English sailors from Nelson's fleet,
> Americans from New Bedford, Italians, Dutch, and Mulattos from St Helena and South
> Africa. English is the native tongue, albeit a slightly strange, preserved Georgian dialect
> with a Biblical flavour, laced with a few early Americanisms.

The 1996 edition of the *Lonely Planet Guide to Antarctica* (p 284) describes the dialect as
follows:

> The islanders' somewhat unusual speech is characterized by slow enunciation; their
> accent is thought to resemble that of English spoken in parts of Britain during the early
> 19th century.

And here is how the dialect is described in a website dedicated to the birdlife of Tristan
(http://www.oceanwanderers.com/TristandaCunha.html):

> Tristan Islanders speak a distinct dialect of English that reflects their origins in Georgian
> England but is also laced with a few early Americanisms, again reflecting the influences of
> early sailors.

These quotations illustrate the commonly held assumption that remote dialects like Tristan
da Cunha English represent older forms of English. Indeed, most people take it for
granted that the sounds, words and grammatical structures of isolated dialects are
untouched by the course of time. In this view, Tristan English represents a form of English

as spoken about 200 years ago. If this were really true, then hearing a Tristanian speak would be like stepping into a time machine and encountering the state of the English language in the 1820s.

The myth about dialects frozen in time and space is remarkably widespread and persistent. Specialists who study such dialects and work with geographically isolated communities encounter it frequently. For instance, linguists who study the English dialect spoken in the Appalachian Mountains – the mountain range in the eastern part of the United States known as "America's first frontier" – hear time and time again that Shakespearean English has been preserved there to the present day. An American dialectologist, Walt Wolfram, was encouraged by friends and colleagues to investigate the dialect of English spoken on Ocracoke, an island on the Outer Banks, about 20 miles off the North Carolina coast, because the fishermen there speak "just like Queen Elizabeth did".

The "Olde English" myth seems to be only one of the numerous stereotypes dwellers of more urban places have about isolated communities. The reasoning underlying such views is simple: seclusion from mainstream communities automatically results in a slowing–down process and conservatism, and manifests itself in a general sense of backwardness in all domains of everyday life, such as dress, traditions, songs, folklore, and, last but not least, language. So how much of this myth is really true? Do communities like Tristan really speak a "slightly strange, preserved Georgian dialect", or is it just a popular myth that cannot be upheld when we look at their speech patterns more carefully? Indeed, some recent linguistic research suggests the opposite, namely that dialects far away from the mainstream have the potential to develop grammatical structures or sounds very quickly, and that isolated speakers may in fact accelerate language change. For instance, the inhabitants of Smith Island, located in the Chesapeake Bay southeast of Washington DC, have over the last few decades extended their use of *weren't* to contexts where standard English has *wasn't*, so that they say "the dog *weren't* outside" or "she *weren't* at home" (Schilling-Estes 2002). Younger Smith islanders use this pattern much more frequently than older members of the community, resulting in rather abrupt language change in a relatively isolated community. Such findings suggest that isolated speakers may speed up language change when they have no outside influence to hold them back, rather than adhering to the speech ways of their parents and grandparents. Given the remoteness of the South Atlantic Islands, the Tristan da Cunha community is ideal to answer these questions. To what extent have the Tristanians preserved the original structures and sounds transplanted to the island? Is it early 19th century English, as some visitors or travel writers claim? Or rather, have they independently developed new sounds and structures?

As so often, stereotypes are partially right and partially wrong, and the truth is somewhere in the middle. We are only now beginning to understand the complexity of the grammar and sound system of Tristan da Cunha English, and recent research findings reveal both that archaic usages have been retained and that new forms have also been created. It is certainly true that isolated communities may preserve words or grammatical structures that were once widespread and have now died out in mainstream dialects. For instance, the word *qualmish*, applied to a variety of stomach disorders, used to be widespread in British English but disappeared from usage some time in the 19th century. On Tristan da Cunha, however, *qualmish* survives and continues to be used (and confuses doctors new to the island who have no idea what's wrong when their patients complain that they feel a bit *qualmish*). Not only are old words retained; archaic sounds or grammatical features are also found. For example, the Tristanians have preserved features that were once common in the British Isles but are now rare, such as the insertion of a so–called "hypercorrect h" (in words such as *egg*, pronounced as 'hegg', or *expedition* as 'hexpedition'), or the pronunciation of words like *hair* or *share* as 'here' or 'sheer'. (The Tristanians 'sheer' their longboats between them and have their 'here' cut, and a similar usage also survives in New Zealand English.) Another sound archaism which is prominent in present-day Tristan da Cunha English is the interchange of /v/ and /w/ in words such as *village* (pronounced 'willage'), *very* ('wery') and *volcano* ('wolcano').[1] We find evidence of this interchange in Charles Dickens' novels, for instance in direct speech samples from 19th century Cockney English:

> I had a reg'lar new fit o' clothes that mornin', gen'l'men of the jury, said Sam, and that was a *wery* partickler and uncommon circumstance *vith* me in those days … bein' only eyes, you see, my *wision's* limited (Charles Dickens, *The Pickwick Papers*, chapter 34)

An archaic grammatical feature still maintained on Tristan is the usage of forms of *be* for *have* in perfect structures ('she must not *be* checked it very good' or 'that's the largest fish *I'm* caught', see below), and perhaps also the usage of *done* as an aspect marker (as in 'she say she's *done* sent the photographs'). All these features, once widespread in the motherland, have largely died out and survive mainly in isolated post–colonial communities. In a sense, then, isolated dialects represent an ideal laboratory to explore some selected features of earlier periods of a given language, and Tristan da Cunha English allows us to identify and look into a number of language changes that have occurred in the meantime. At the same time, it is simplistic, and in fact quite incorrect, to assume that people in remote places speak exactly like their founding fathers and Queen Victoria did. The Tristanians have preserved older elements, but a simple "Olde English" view fails to recognise how complex and intricate language change really is. In fact, we will see below that the dialect has undergone entirely new changes and developed exclusively Tristanian features that are unknown to all other dialects in the English-speaking world. Consequently, the "Olde English" myth is partially right, and geographic seclusion may lead to the survival of archaic features that have long ago died out in more mainstream communities. On the other hand, being isolated from other places may also result in the evolution of new and totally unique forms.

So what do people think about this form of English, and what have outsiders said about this dialect with which they are unfamiliar? Where do people think it is from, and how do they describe it? We have already encountered a view that it is "London dockland English", i.e. that it represents Cockney English. With what other forms of English has the "Tristan Slang" been associated, and what can these observations teach us about the dialect?

3.2 Tristan da Cunha English – the unknown dialect

Today, the Tristanians spend more time than ever in the outside world. They become increasingly aware of the distinctiveness of their dialect (as evidenced by the comment of former Chief Islander Harold Green at the beginning of this chapter), and they find that visitors or eavesdroppers wonder about their unfamiliar way of speaking. When in South Africa or the UK, the Tristanians often find themselves in situations where people inquire about this unfamiliar accent they just cannot place. Some of these comments are biased and unfair; for instance, when the Tristanians spent the 1961–63 "volcano years" in the UK, a psychologist analysed the speech behaviour of the children and concluded that most of them had a language impairment. Other people indulge in the stereotype that isolated speakers have small vocabularies (which is completely wrong, as people who had vivid discussions with Tristanians will gladly confirm), or worse still, that they do not speak at all. An American journalist complained in his TV documentary that "on Tristan, not even the dogs would speak to me", and a Swiss journalist described the Tristanians as "monosyllabic" and suggested that their birthdays parties are boring since "what is there to talk about when nothing ever happens?" Obviously, it had not crossed the minds of these people that the Tristanians are embarrassed when visitors observe them constantly, and that they simply do not feel at ease when surrounded by visitors carrying cameras,

---

[1]   This is also a feature of St Helenian English as well as of the English Creole of St Kitts and other islands of the north-eastern Caribbean (Baker 1999).

microphones and note pads (this also has implications for dialect research, as will be seen below). Most people are not in the mood for talking when being observed by nosy strangers anyway, and this is true on Tristan da Cunha as well as in probably all communities. The fact that Tristanians do not speak much in the presence of expatriates does not mean that they do not speak much among themselves.

But back to the question how observers place Tristan da Cunha English. Some visitors have claimed that it is basically a language of its own, since they were not able to understand the locals' speech. For instance, a South African visitor who spent time on the island in the mid-1980s told us: "When I first went to the island I did not understand a word they said. I just laughed when they laughed. Yeah, I could have laughed when they told me their grandmother died and I wouldn't have known". By the same token, several expatriate teachers reported that they had considerable problems of understanding the local dialect. Rhoda Downer, a former headmistress at the local school, wrote in 1957: "Sometimes I have to make the schoolchildren repeat sentences slowly, before I can be sure of the meaning. They have two distinct languages, and they have forgotten school speech during the holiday" (Evans 1994:288). This view is shared by Jim Flint, the head teacher on Tristan da Cunha from 1963 to 1965 (just after the 'Volcano Years'). He too thought that the islanders had a "Dickensian speech" and wrote: "the children simply speak two languages – School English and Island English" (Evans 1994:274). They both report that, when among themselves, the Tristanians speak in a notably different manner and can barely be understood. At the same time, this contrasts with the islanders' own perception of their dialect. Even though they have many amusing stories to tell about those 'station fellas' who have no idea what the locals are talking about, the Tristanians regard their dialect as a form of English and nothing else.

When abroad, Tristanians find that quite often people who have never heard their dialect before are curious about their origin and venture a guess, saying: "oh, I bet you must be from …". When we look at some descriptions and guesses people have made, it is quite striking that observers do not agree at all on the whereabouts of this mysterious accent. The comments of casual observers or tourists vary widely, and a few selected quotes may serve to illustrate this. Tristan da Cunha English is perceived to be ...

… *American English:*
All the people here speak English slightly Yankeefied. (Rev. Erwin Dodgson, 1882, in Evans, 1994).

… *British English:*
The speech of most of the community is slow and similar to a west country dialect.
(Captain Harold Pearce, 1904)[2]

There were vowels as in English north country dialect. (Dr Barlois, 1937)[2]

[A form of] English which went out of fashion in London's docklands in the first years of Queen Victoria's reign. (Arne Falk–Rønne, 1967)

…*"Mixed" English:*
Three different brogues, one resembling the speech of the St Helenas, one having the American twang, and the other strongly reminding me of a west of England dialect.
(Dr Hammond Tooke, 1906)[2]

Their speech shows traces of American, Scotch and Cockney influences. (Allan Crawford, 1941)

Tristan English has echoes of Dickensian Cockney, Australian, Afrikaans and American.
(Michael Moynihan, 1962)[2]

Their accents combine elements of Scots and Afrikaans in a strange, slow drawl.
(Daniel Booy, 1957)

It is a strange mixture of Australian and Cockney. (Adam Raphael, 1966)[2]

---

2   Quotations from Pearce, Barlois, Tooke, Moynihan, and Raphael all come from documents and newspaper cuttings held in Saint Louis University's Tristan da Cunha Coollection.

There is no consensus at all, and Tristan da Cunha English is interpreted as anything from Cockney to American and Australian English or as a mixture of these. This illustrates well how confused we are when encountering a dialect that is unfamiliar to us – we obviously recognise it as English but just cannot figure out where it is spoken. Some recent linguistic research used speech samples from Tristan da Cunha English, and individuals in the USA and New Zealand were asked where in the English-speaking world they would place this dialect. Participants listened to the tape-recorded speech of six Tristanians, born between 1906 and 1978. They were given a questionnaire where it said "United Kingdom or Ireland, namely …" or "Outside the British Isles, namely …", and instructed to note which variety of English around the World they thought they were listening to. Answers ranged from Canada, Ireland, and south-western England, to South Africa and Australia. On a personal note, Karen Lavarello–Schreier has experienced such confusion many times and has a story to tell about what people think where she is from – Americans think she is from England or Australia, in England the people believe she is from South Africa, South Africans assume her to be from Australia or New Zealand, and when she lived in New Zealand people usually thought she was from Canada, the USA, England or South Africa. Tristan da Cunha English seems to be spoken everywhere and nowhere. So what is it really? What dialects of English does it derive from and how can we retrace its ancestry?

3.3 Where does Tristan da Cunha English come from?

There was no indigenous population when the military garrison was established on Tristan da Cunha in 1816; the only inhabitant, Tomasso Corri, died soon after the soldiers arrived. As a result, the community's founders brought their own dialects with them and did not come into contact with pre-existing languages. Two centuries ago, there was no such thing as Tristan da Cunha English, and now a few hundred people speak it natively. This raises several questions, namely: Exactly how and when did the local dialect develop? How did it form and evolve, and who formed it? Does it historically derive from one variety of English only (for instance, Scottish English), which it still preserves in its more or less original state? Or, alternatively, is it the result of mixing of several different dialects, in that it has selected words, sounds and grammatical features from several if not all dialects that were transplanted to the island?

One way to approach this question is with reference to what is generally known as the "founder effect". The idea is that the dialects spoken by the founders of a new colony leave a permanent imprint and influence the future development of the newly forming variety. Whoever comes first, whoever founds the colony, hands down their speech to the generations to come, and the dialect(s) of the pioneers serve(s) as a role model for their offspring. So what happened on Tristan da Cunha? Did William Glass, the founder and well–respected patriarch of the colony, hand down Scottish English to the first generations of native Tristanians, or did the women from St Helena pass their English on to their children? Or did all these dialects merge, and did Tristan English adopt features from British English, American English, *and* St Helenian English? To answer this, we obviously need to know the exact geographic origins of the founders of the colony. Once we know what dialects were transplanted to the island, we can match the features of Tristan English with features of the putative donor dialects, which allows us to analyse processes of feature selection that occurred when the first generations of native Tristanians were born. What were the model dialects for the first generations of children born on the island? As we saw in Chapter 1, the four different founding groups were British, American, European (two Danes, a Dutchman, and two Italians), and the group of women from St Helena. Which of them was most influential linguistically?

The British and American settlers had mixed backgrounds. The first settlers came from the British Isles, namely from Southwest England (John Nankivel and Samuel Burnell), London ("Old Dick" Riley), Sussex (Thomas Swain), Yorkshire (Alexander Cotton) and from the Scottish Lowlands (William Glass). The origins of the settlers are given in Table 1 below, with the cross symbol (+) indicating that the individual died on Tristan da Cunha. Whereas the origins of the British colonizers are well documented, considerably less is known about the origins of the American settlers. Captain Andrew Hagan, the most influential member of this group, was born in New London, Massachusetts, but the origins of his companions are unknown (particularly those of Samuel Johnson and William Daley). Their professions may give us some vital clues though. All of them were whalers and sealers, and this suggests that they may have come from areas with a strong whaling tradition (i.e. coastal New England), rather than from traditional farming communities elsewhere. We also know that several of them were familiar with the people on Tristan da Cunha, as they had visited the island on previous occasions (the Glass family particularly had links with New England: in the 1830s and 1840s, several daughters of William Glass married American whalers and joined them to live in the United States). The question of origins aside, the Americans had less influence on the dialect than the British settlers. First, the arrival of William Glass and his companions predated the settlement of the Americans. Even though two Americans were short–term members of the community in the early 1820s, the first permanent settlers from the US arrived only in the 1830s, when the colony was already founded and established. Second, the Americans resided on the island for shorter periods and most of them left the island after a few years. This suggests that the most important "founder effects" and language contributions in this early period came from the British.

British and American settlers on Tristan da Cunha from 1817 to 1850

British			American		
Name	Origins	Residence	Name	Origins	Residence
William Glass	Kelso, Scotland	1816–1853+	Thomas Fotheringham	USA	1820–1823
Samuel Burnell	Plymouth (Devonshire)	1816–1820	John Turnbull	USA	1820–1823
John Nankivel	Plymouth	1816–1823	Samuel Johnson	USA	1833–1847
Richard Riley	Wapping/ East London	1820–1857	William Daley	USA	1836–1857
Alexander Cotton	Hull	1821–1865+	Thomas Rogers	USA	1837–1839
Stephen White	England	1821–1826	Andrew Hagan	New London, Mass.	1849–1898+
George Peart	Britain	1825–1837			
Thomas Swain	Hastings	1826–1862+			

Another group we need to consider consists of the settlers who did not speak English as a native language. The Dane Peter Petersen settled on Tristan da Cunha in 1825, and Peter Møller, from Denmark also, and Pieter Willem Groen, from Katwijik in Holland, arrived in 1836. Andrea Repetto and Gaetano Lavarello, the two Italians, were the last non–Anglophone settlers and arrived in 1892. Another member of the community who perhaps did not speak English natively was the wife of Governor Glass, Maria (née Leenders). Augustus Earle, the castaway artist who met her in person, described her as a "Cape Creole" and his portrait of the community suggests that she was of dark complexion. According to other reports, the father of Maria Glass was a Dutch–speaking Boer and her mother a non–white South African whose origins are not specified. Maria

Glass most probably grew up in the Dutch–speaking community of Cape Town at a time when South Africa was sharply divided between the colonists of Dutch and British descent. It is quite possible that she spoke an early form of Afrikaans in her youth and only learnt English when she met William Glass, her future husband, in 1814. Consequently, the non-Anglophone settlers had the following native languages: Afrikaans and Dutch (and we should add that 200 years ago, they were not as distinct as they are now), Danish, and Italian. How much influence did they have on the dialect? Is Tristan da Cunha English really similar to Afrikaans, as some visitors have suggested?

These languages certainly contributed a number of words (see below); as for sounds and grammar, though, the linguistic influence of the languages other than English was not extensive, and probably restricted to a handful of features. Reverend William Taylor noted that English was the only language spoken on Tristan da Cunha in the 1850s. Pieter Willem Groen, the most influential member in this group, was highly proficient in English; several Captains who traded and bartered with him reported that his command of English was "impressive" and "excellent". Similar reports exist for Andrea Repetto, whose Italian gallantry was much appreciated by Mrs Barrow, the wife of the missionary who served on the island from 1906 to 1909. She wrote that when stepping aboard the dinghy, she was greeted by Andrea Repetto with the following words: "Be careful, Madam, it not very comfortable for a lady" (Barrow 1910). The non–Anglophone settlers were thus proficient enough to communicate with the settlers from the British Isles, America and St Helena; they adapted to the English–speaking members of the community, and not vice versa. Not only did they speak English, they also strongly identified with the colony's British character and were keen on integrating themselves into the community. Pieter Willem Groen converted to Presbyterianism (and so did Andrea Repetto some 60 years later), and he also anglicized his name to Peter William Green (his descendants on the island today are the Greens, not the Groens). At the same time, we know for a fact that the non-British settlers continued to speak their native languages with each other, and particularly the Italians taught their relatives some words. When we revisited Tristan da Cunha in September 2002, for instance, we were amazed to find that Gertie Lavarello, then aged 96, could still count from one to ten in Italian, more than 50 years after the death of Gaetano Lavarello, her father-in-law.

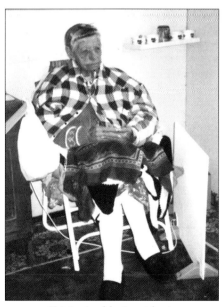

Tristan's oldest resident,
Gertie Lavarello, at the age of 96

The last group we need to consider consists of the women who arrived from St Helena in 1827. We know very little about them. All of them were born on the island of St Helena, even though Reverend William Taylor noted in his 1851 census that one of them had English parents and another one an English father. At least some of them were of mixed ethnicity, and logbook entries and medical reports mention that the Tristan community was racially diverse. In 1906, for instance, Dr Hammond Tooke conducted a medical examination on Tristan da Cunha and described the community as follows:

> With regard to physical appearance, the Hagan, Glass and Rogers type, have fair complexions and are almost Scandinavian in appearance. The Swains and Greens are generally more swarthy, yet most are unmistakably European. Samuel Swain with his black hair and bushy whiskers is quite the darkest of all, but one could scarcely regard him as black. One or two of the women showed traces of black descent in their hair and complexion.[3]

Perhaps some of these women were former slaves who left St Helena in hope of a better life elsewhere. (This is what Jan Brander, the Dutch historian of Tristan da Cunha, suggests). We do not know if there is any truth to this claim, but with effect from Christmas Day 1818, the Governor and Council of St Helena abolished slavery and decreed that all children born of slave women were free citizens. This law would have made it possible for slaves to leave St Helena, particularly those with young children born after that date (which some of these women had). So, even though the exact nature of their dialects is unknown, it seems clear that they were important members of the community. The women had a predominant position in child rearing and were the last female newcomers in the 19th century. They were in a particularly influential position in the 1840s and 1850s, when their husbands were employed on American whaling ships and left the islands for considerable periods of time. And of course, the women were also crucial in keeping the community together after the 1885 lifeboat disaster. Therefore, all this indicates that St Helenian English, in whatever form, contributed significantly to the new local Tristan dialect.

Unfortunately, very little is known about the local dialect of English that developed on St Helena. The limited socio-historical and linguistic information available suggest that it was formed in a context of intense language contact, which involved predominantly south-eastern British English and several languages of Africa and Asia. The latter were brought to the island by slaves who were imported by the East India Company from the 1660s onwards. None of the languages of the former slaves survive on the island today. However, it is interesting to note that contemporary St Helenian English bears some striking parallels with Caribbean English Creoles.[4] Creole languages typically develop when speakers of mutually unintelligible languages are brought into sudden, sustained contact, very often under the auspices of slavery. In societies using slave labour, the Creole language which emerged usually had a vocabulary derived mainly from the colonizers' language (Dutch, French, Portuguese, or English) with only a small percentage of words from the languages of the slaves. But stronger influence of the latter languages can frequently be found in the pronunciation and grammar of the Creole language. Consider for instance the following report of direct speech on St Helena, observed by a Miss Doveton, who visited the island in the 1870s. She had a conversation with a local "Negro Boatman", as she called him, and wrote down his very words in her travel accounts:[5]

> Berry bad, massa. Lib heself, no like see anybody else do de same. Tink berry good ting spose one big fish swaller he up, all same Jonah dat de bishop tell de darkies bout turra

---

3   This quotation is taken from a copy of Dr Tooke's original report, which is held in the Peter Munch Collection at Saint Louis University.

4   A pioneering list of these is given by Hancock 1991.

5   We would like to thank Philip Baker for bringing this document to our attention.

day. Spose you ask he 'How he like St Helena for lib in?' he say 'Berry bad place?'. Spose ask he 'How like de peoble?' he say 'More bad; no lady, gentleman got'. He no got one good word for anybody, anyting. Peoble no like him too. Turra day massa gubner he gib gran ception Queen's buf-day.

This brief passage contains several typical Creole features. To mention but a few: the realisation of the English sound /v/ as b (_berry_ 'very', _lib_ 'live'), the realisation of the English /th/ sounds as t (_tink_ 'think', _ting_ 'thing') and d (_dat_ 'that'), the reduction of word-final consonants and the clipping of unstressed first syllables (_gran_' _ception_ 'grand reception'), _no_ as a general marker of negativity (_peoble no like him_), and the infinitive of a verb with past reference (_tell_ instead of _told_, as in '_de bishop tell de darkies_'). Even though St Helenian English has not yet been subject to serious linguistic research, reports such as this make it clear that a Creole was spoken on the island until fairly recently, and the question is to what extent Creoles shaped the historical evolution of the local dialect on St Helena.

Language varieties which potentially contributed to Tristan da Cunha English

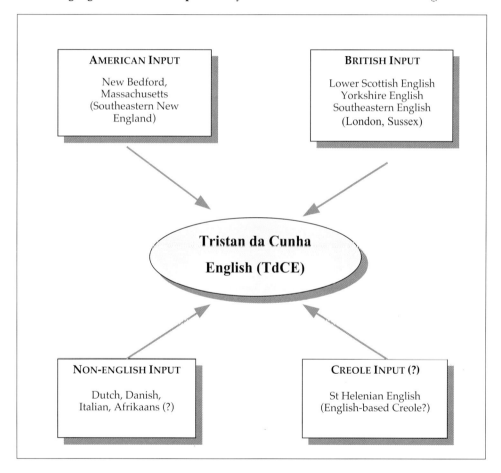

But to return to the status of Tristan da Cunha English, the picture which begins to emerge is that a number of distinct dialects of English were transplanted to the island. The Americans and Europeans were not as significant as the immigrants from the British Isles and St Helena, and there were two main influential groups: the British group, led by William Glass from Kelso, Scotland, and the St Helenian women. The question is consequently how British and St Helenian dialects of English interacted when the community developed, and what dialect served as a role model for the first children born on the island. Did one dialect make it, or did all of them merge in the speech of the first generations?

3.4 Reconstructing the history of Tristan da Cunha English

The modern form of Tristan da Cunha English gives us clues as to how it formed originally and what exactly happened when all these dialects were brought to the island in the first half of the 19th century. When analysing the dialect as it is spoken today, we can pinpoint some structures to different areas of origin and thus speculate not only who brought this grammatical form or sound to Tristan da Cunha, but also which of the various input dialects was more influential than others. However, such analyses are not always as straightforward as we might wish. For example, the birth certificate of William Glass shows that he was born in Kelso in the Scottish Lowlands in 1786 and, from Augustus Earle's narrative, we know that Glass spent his youth there. However, some caution is needed because of the often substantial period of time between settlers leaving their place of origin and their ultimate arrival in Tristan. Almost all the male settlers had a strong nautical background, and some of them had spent several decades at sea before reaching the island. Nobody knows what happened to their speech while they were working on the ships. They would surely have acquired a good deal of nautical vocabulary. Indeed, Augustus Earle's (1832) account refers to the "particular seamen's phraseology" of William Glass and his colleagues.

It is perfectly plausible to assume that they underwent language shift and modified their native dialects. The contact situations on board the sailing ships may on occasion lead to accommodation and have a permanent effect, which was arguably further reinforced by interaction with people from coastal areas. The theory of so-called 'nautical English' is by no means new, and the American linguist John Reinecke argued in the 1930s already that sailors may have developed their own pidgin languages and, by doing so, played an important role in the diffusion of such varieties. He wrote: "One of the most favourable situations for the formation of such dialects is found aboard merchant vessels, which ply the seven seas and ship large numbers of foreign sailors" (1937:142), which would strengthen this point. On the other hand, as we shall see below, Tristan da Cunha English has properties that can be specifically traced to one or several of the areas where the settlers came from, and this indicates that the donor dialects did indeed bear some resemblances with the settlers' dialects of origin. Therefore, 'nautical English', if that was what the settlers spoke, was not as strong as to eradicate all founder effects, and a few examples will illustrate this.

First of all, one area where most settlers left a legacy is the vocabulary. The lexicon of Tristan da Cunha English reflects the social history of the community in several ways, and it is as if each group of settlers wanted to add their own little bit to the local dialect. The majority of the word stock is British and/or St Helenian, but we also find words that have entered the lexicon from other sources, including Dutch and/or Afrikaans, American English, and perhaps Danish and Italian. Thus, the word stock of Tristan da Cunha English reflects the range of dialects and languages transported to the island. We have already mentioned that the Tristanians have preserved the archaic usage of *qualmish* for 'sick in the stomach', which reflects a British heritage. Similarly, the word *dicelen*, the local word for 'thistle', has its origin in regional dialects of British English, since this word, pronounced [daɪslən], is attested in Devon and Cornwall. Two of the colony's founders, Thomas Burnell and Samuel Nankivel, were stonemasons from Plymouth, and *dicel* was almost certainly brought to Tristan da Cunha via these two settlers, thus representing a legacy of Southwestern dialectal British English. On the other hand, Tristan da Cunha English also has words that are unknown in the British Isles, for instance *kooibietjie*, pronounced 'coy-beech-ee', which is from Afrikaans and means 'take a little nap', 'sleep a little while' (from Afrikaans *kooi* 'bed' and *bietjie* 'a little bit'), or *molly*, an abbreviation of *mollymawk* which derives from Dutch *mallemok*, 'albatross'. In addition, Tristan da Cunha English has words that sound familiar to English ears but whose local meanings are unknown in the British Isles, such as the word *catfish*. Outsiders usually think this refers to a true fish species when they hear Tristanians say that they are "using catfish for bait", but they are confused when they find out that a Tristan *catfish* is not a fish at all but an octopus. (The same meaning is reported in the Caribbean, on St Helena, and in the speech of Cape Coloureds in South Africa, which suggests that this term may have reached Tristan da Cunha by more than one route).[6] Another interesting usage is the verb *to stop*, which does not mean 'come to a halt' but 'stay' or 'live with somebody' (you *stop* in someone's home, instead of staying in it; and you *stop* in England, instead of living in England – "that's the fella what stop with Herbert", as they would say on Tristan). On the other hand, distinctive words may also have been created on the island itself. One of the most common fish species in Tristan waters is called the *fivefinger*, a name that has not been reported anywhere else and may well have been coined by the islanders. (It has dark stripes along the sides, as if five fingers had scratched it). At the same time, technological inventions or newly imported products have led to the adoption of words from other languages (particularly from Afrikaans). For instance, recently imported goods from South Africa led to the adoption of words such as *braai* 'barbecue', *boerewors* 'sausage', and *bakki* 'truck' . Dutch and Afrikaans – since both were brought to Tristan and are closely related, it is quite difficult to determine which of these is the source – also contributed words in the domains of the household (*bankie* 'bench', *bredie* 'meat and vegetable stew'), fishing terminology (*snoek*, *steenbras* are fish species in Tristan waters, and perhaps also *klipfish*, even though this might alternatively be of Danish origin - see the Glossary for more information), everyday life (*kappi* 'bonnet', *lekker* 'delicious', and *kraal* 'sheep pen'), and we also find some Italian food terms in the local dialect. Perhaps it is hearing these words that led some observers to assume that Tristan English is a form of Afrikaans. However, a handful of words do not make a dialect, and the contribution of Afrikaans to Tristanian English is marginal at best.

We also find that existing English words are re-used for new terms in Tristan English. Some of the founders used existing words to refer to similar items they had no word for. For instance, the word *canary* is used to refer to the 'Tristan bunting' (*Nesospiza acunhae*), whose primary habitat now is Nightingale Island. Words were also reused in the domain of the household. For example, refrigerators are called *coolers* on Tristan da Cunha (which causes great confusion when they are ordered in Cape Town; South Africans have no idea what the order is and it has occurred on occasion that the wrong article was sent). By the same token, only a few Tristanians use the word 'ketchup'; instead, *mato sauce* (with a clipped first syllable, pronounced something like 'muh-dee') is the common term on the island. A special word in Tristan da Cunha English is *canteen*, which is used to refer to the island's only general store. This usage of *canteen* can be explained historically: the Tristanians did not have a local shopping place until the soldiers arrived in 1942. They then built a small general store for the patronage of the army personnel (which in military jargon is a *canteen*). When the naval station was withdrawn, the store remained for the local population, and with it stayed the name. The words *store* and *supermarket* are hardly

---

6   The Oxford English dictionary (OED) has the following two entries for 'catfish':
     1 A name given to various fishes (such as the wolf-fish and the North-American fresh-water fish, with specimen dated from 1662 and 1697).
     2 The *cuttle-fish* or other *cephalod* 1678 Phillips, "catfish, a sort of fish in some parts of the West Indies, so-called from the Round-head, and large glaring Eyes, by which they are discovered in the Concavities in the Rocks." 1753. Baker in Phil. Trans. L. 785: "Sea Polypi are frequent in the Mediterranean .. A different species came from the West Indies, where it is called a Cat-fish."
        The chronology of these attestations suggests that the word originated in the West Indies, and spread from there, perhaps via slaves or indentured labourers, to South Africa, and on to St Helena and Tristan da Cunha.

used, and Tristanians may be the only speakers of English who would say a sentence such as 'mato sauce is on sale in the canteen today'.

Finally, an additional source for the Tristan da Cunha English lexicon was American English, and distinctive words were picked up from Captain Hagan and his companions as well as from the American whalers who frequented the area in the 1840s and 1850s. An American heritage is found in words such as *gulch*, the contracted form *tater* ("potato'), the use of *mad* for 'angry' and *I guess* for 'I reckon', and perhaps also in the second person plural pronoun *y'all* ('y'all is watching too much out of the window').

In terms of vocabulary, the local dialect represents a cosmopolitan mix of features that reflects the international atmosphere of its settlement history. As for its sound system and grammar, however, it resembles mainly British and St Helenian English. For instance, the dialect is very unlike General American English, as Tristanians would not pronounce the *r* in *car* or *park*, and they would pronounce words like *grass* or *path* with an *a* sound as in *father* and not as in *bad*. Analysing Tristan da Cunha English as it is spoken today, we can trace a number of structures to dialects spoken in England, Scotland and on St Helena, and this suggests that it is a mixed form of English and that features were selected from several founders' dialects (in different proportions, of course). Whereas some features are found in Scotland but not in any other dialect represented on Tristan da Cunha, others are reported on St Helena and not in British English. One feature that was fairly widespread in British English until about 1800 was the usage of *be* as an auxiliary verb (in contexts where contemporary English uses *have*), the so-called 'perfective *be*'. Tristanians very often use *be* instead of *have*, as in 'she must *be* got no work to do', 'I'*m* checked the parcels already', or '*is* they gone to the patches?'. This usage has a long-standing historical continuity in the British Isles, and is found, for instance, in the works of Geoffrey Chaucer and William Shakespeare:

> 'Upon a day bifel that he for his desport *is went* into the feeldes hym to pleye' (*The Tale of Melibee*)
> 'Macduff *is fled* to England' (*Macbeth*)
> 'Thou told'st me they *were stolen* into this wood' (*A Midsummer Night's Dream*)

English grammar varied between *be* and *have* for a long time, and *have* only became established towards the end of the 18th century. The fact that the Tristanians have preserved this feature therefore reflects a British heritage (and identifies this feature as a legacy of William Glass, 'Old Dick' Riley, or Thomas Swain). At the same time, it emphasises what we have mentioned above, namely that isolated dialects are likely to maintain some relic features that have disappeared in more mainstream communities. Usage of *be* for *have* has almost died out in the British Isles and is found in a few areas only, such as the English Fens that separate East Anglia from the eastern Midlands (that is, in areas that are comparatively isolated as well).

Another feature found in the British Isles until quite recently is the insertion of /h/ in words that begin with a stressed vowel, which is sometimes referred to as hypercorrect /h/ or as /h/ insertion. This feature too makes an appearance in English literature, for instance in Charles Dickens' novels:

> 'If they wos a pair o' patent double million magnifyin' gas microscopes of *hextra* power, p'raps I might be able to see through a flight o' stairs and a deal door' (Charles Dickens, *The Pickwick Papers*, 1837).

Retention of /h/ insertion is one of the most salient characteristics of the Tristanians' way of speaking, and since it so noticeable it is much commented on by visitors. In the book in which he relates his experiences on Tristan da Cunha during the 1937-38 Norwegian expedition, Allan Crawford (1941) refers to the "Georgian" appearance of the dialect, and mentions that the Tristanians often say that they live on a 'highland' instead of on an 'island'. In the case of /h/ retention too, Tristan da Cunha English has preserved a feature that has practically disappeared elsewhere, and this allows researchers to investigate and understand speech patterns that have gone elsewhere.

With the aim of reconstructing the formation and evolution of Tristan da Cunha English, we need to focus on variables that can be traced to one different donor variety to this dialect, and not to others. Ideally, we would pinpoint a given structure in a given input dialect (for instance, Scottish English), explain why this particular feature was selected and not others present in the original mixture situation, and thus retrace the ancestry and history of the local dialect. Practically, however, this is not always feasible for a number of reasons. First of all, it occurs quite often that features can be traced to several inputs and that they thus have multiple origins (in fact, linguistic research on similar scenarios in Fiji or in South Africa has shown that features are more likely to be selected when they are found in more than one of the dialects in contact). Second, sometimes we may not have reliable historical information to track a given feature in an earlier form of a dialect (for instance, late 18th century Cockney) or we may have very little or no evidence at all (early 19th century Saint Helenian English). This may make it impossible to delineate the origins of language features. Third, all dialects are subject to language change and their sounds, words and grammatical structures are in a constant process of transformation. Therefore, a given feature may originate in a donor dialect but then undergo additional developments that camouflage its heritage. One example here would be perfective *be* in Lumbee English, a dialect of English that developed among Native Americans of the Lumbee tribe in south-eastern North Carolina (Wolfram 1996). Like the Tristanians, the Lumbee have preserved the usage of 'I'm seen it' as well, but they have specialised this usage so that they use forms of perfective *be* predominantly with first person singular persons (they are quite likely to say 'I'*m* had three heart attacks', but would rarely say 'you'*re* had three heart attacks'), and with contracted verb forms (they are much more likely to say 'I'*m* watered the flowers' than 'I *am* watered the flowers'). In combination with the considerations discussed above, additional developments of this type add to the complexity of the task, and it is very often not possible to determine whether a given feature represents a true relic form, whether it underwent additional developments, or whether it originated in this particular locale.

Nevertheless, a feature analysis can give us vital clues as to how Tristan da Cunha English formed, and a brief discussion of a few selected variables illustrate how we can make use of linguistic information to shed light on the development of this dialect. The first of these structures is the type of present tense concord. Standard English marks the third person singular only with an –s suffix ('she dances', 'he paints', whereas all other subjects have no marking in present tense ('I go', 'they sing', etc.). This type of present tense concord is by far the most widespread in English around the world, but it is not the only one. For instance, some dialects in the British Isles and elsewhere have differential patterns. On of these alternative marking systems is the (optional) suffixation of an –s marker with all persons, as in "I says" or "we sings", which is found in regional dialects in southwestern and northern England. Another pattern is –s marking with third person singular subjects (just as in standard English), but also with third person plural subjects and plural nouns (as in "they goes" and "the dogs barks"). Following the American linguist Michael Montgomery, who analysed tense marking in earlier forms of British and American dialects of English, this marking system is commonly called 'Northern Concord' (since it was particularly frequent in Northern English and Scottish dialects). A third pattern has no marking at all, in that no subject receives –s marking, not even the third person singular, which is realised as "when it rain" or "he walk" (this is found in East Anglian English, particularly in Norfolk and Suffolk, African-American English and also in English-based Pidgins and Creoles around the world). There are thus four different systems of present tense concord:

- A standard-like system, with –s marking for third person singulars only

- A system where all grammatical persons and plural NPs have –s suffixation (e.g. 'I takes', 'we works', in southwestern and northern England)
- A system where only the third singular and plural persons as well as plural NPs are marked (e.g. in 'they goes', the dogs barks', the 'Northern Concord' system)
- A system with no overt tense marking, i.e. no –s suffixation at all (e.g. 'it rain', found in East Anglia, African American English, and pidginised/creolised forms of English)

Even though these patterns are of course not neatly separated from one dialect region to the next and may co-occur in one area or even within the same speaker, they nevertheless can be by and large attributed to certain dialects. Therefore, since Tristan da Cunha English originated in a context that involved several dialects of British English, the selection of one of these patterns should give us clues concerning its heritage and evolution of the local dialect. Which of these patterns was selected?

It turns out that the present tense concord we find in Tristan da Cunha English today has no British heritage at all. The Tristanians have no overt present tense marking, and no –s suffix. Not only do the say "I go" and "they write", but also "the dog bark" and "she wait outside". Even though some of the younger and more mobile members of the community have –s marking occasionally, this pattern is very robust on Tristan da Cunha; elderly Tristanians lack this marker entirely and have no –s in present tense concord. This system is found in the British Isles, namely in the dialect of English spoken in East Anglia, i.e., an area with which Tristan da Cunha has no sociohistorical connections whatsoever. In other words, even though Tristan da Cunha English shares exactly the same feature with a form of British English, there is no direct link between them. On the other hand, St Helenian English has this system, presumably due to the fact that it underwent pidginization and creolization, which suggests that the women from St Helena transplanted and transmitted it to the first generations of native Tristanians in the late 1820s and early 1830s. The fact that the St Helenian input won out is a first indication how influential these women were, both socially and linguistically. The British and American settlers had present tense concord systems that involved some kind of –s marking, either with third person singulars only (the standard pattern) or with other subjects as well (as in 'Northern Concord'). None of these marking patterns survived (or rather: were adopted when the first native speakers of the local dialect selected their features from some of their parents' speech). Put differently, the selection of a system with no –s marking shows that St Helenian English was a fairly influential donor dialect to Tristan da Cunha English.

Another feature that originated in contact with an English Creole, and can thus be pinpointed to non-British sources, is the reduction of word-final consonant clusters. English is unusual in that its sound system allows combinations of consonants, or so-called consonant clusters, to co-occur. Many of the world's languages have no such clusters, and instead have a rigid order of alternating vowels and consonants, in a sequence of consonant-vowel-consonant-vowel (or CVCV). In cases of language contact that involve English, one of the most usual characteristics of the deriving contact variety is that word-final consonant clusters are reduced, and that the last element, or consonant, is omitted. This process is commonly referred to as consonant cluster reduction. What is of importance here is the frequency with which this occurs, because probably all varieties of English, including standard English, have a tendency to reduce consonants (for instance in a word like *Christmas*, where the *t* is usually not pronounced, or in a sentence such as 'she rode past the barn', where the final *t* in *past* tends to be omitted because of the following th sound). All linguistic studies of this phenomenon come to the identical conclusion that such reduction is sensitive both to the status of the word and also to the environment of the cluster. First, the word type affects the frequency of reduction: words that consist of one single element only (such as *past, drift*, or *crisp*) are much more likely to undergo reduction than words that consist of two elements, namely a root and an ending –ed, which marks verbs for past tense (such as *walked, passed*, etc.). Second, the immediately following environment, or sound, affects the rate of word-final consonant reduction as well; when there is a following consonant (such as in 'past the barn' above) then the frequency of reduction is much higher than when the cluster is followed by a vowel ('past a barn') or a pause ('it's half past'). These two effects have been attested with remarkable consistency in every form of English where this feature was investigated.

Most if not all British dialects reduce word-final consonants, but, and this is a very important point, they predominantly reduce clusters a) in words that consist of a single element, and b) that are followed by another consonant. Varieties that originate in contact between English and other languages have much higher rates of consonantal reduction, and they typically have it in all contexts, most importantly in words that take an –ed ending and are followed by a vowel (as in 'she *pass* all her exams last week'), which is very rare in British English. Consonant cluster reduction is thus a diagnostic variable that allows us to check whether English was in contact with other languages, and if so, to assess how strong the impact was. Creole languages typically have very few consonant clusters and prefer the alternation of vowels and consonants, a CVCV structure, which is also found in many of the world's languages. Tristan da Cunha English has a very strong tendency to reduce consonant clusters, not only in words that consist of a single element, but also in words that have a word-final –ed segment. Tristanians would thus not only say 'I can *lif* it' (lift) and 'the book is on the *des*' (desk), but also 'she *walk out* two minutes ago' (walked out) and 'we *live in* a nice house when we was in England' (lived in). In a study of six Tristanians born between 1906 and 1935, which looked into the reduction of –ed endings, it was found that –ed was reduced so often that one might argue that early 20th century Tristan da Cunha English had no past tense marking for regular verbs at all. This obviously cannot represent a British legacy, as no form of British English has or had this feature; it therefore reflects a contact-induced process which again throws light on the speech patterns of the women from St Helena. Not only did they transmit this typical Creole feature to the gradually evolving local dialect on Tristan da Cunha, but they also were influential enough to oust the consonant cluster rates in the speech of the British settlers. In this sense, then, consonant cluster reduction offers vital clues to understand and reconstruct the early developmental stages of Tristan da Cunha English.

We have now looked at two features which can be attributed to certain areas. Perfective *be* is English in origin, but other characteristic structures of Tristan da Cunha English cannot represent a British heritage. The fact that the Tristanians adopted them is a strong indication that Saint Helenian English was a major contributor to a local dialect on Tristan da Cunha, and also that a Creole-type language variety developed on St Helena. However, there also exist cases where such a delimitation is not clear at all, and there are in fact structures where it is almost impossible to pinpoint their origins. One of the possible complications we mentioned above is that sometimes we cannot determine whether a feature is old or new. This may sound odd, but Tristan da Cunha English has at least one feature that could either represent an extraordinary rare relic form from earlier forms of English, or else be dynamic and represent an innovation. This feature is technically referred to as completive *done*. Here the word *done* is used in combination with a verb, as in "she's *done sent* the photograph", and does not function as a past participle ("I have *done* it") or, as found in some (non-standard) forms of English, as an alternative preterit form ("who *done* it?", "that's the only thing I *done*"). Even though its origins are still unclear, this usage of *done* is found in Middle English and Scottish literature, for example, in the works of Richard Maitland and John Dunbar:

'Quhone [When] I haue *done* consider This warldis vanite' (Richard Maitland)
'The fo is chasit, the battle is *done* ceiss, The presone brokin, the jevellouris fleit and flemit' (John Dunbar)

In practically all instances it has a co-occurring auxiliary, which is mostly *have* and very seldom *be*. English-based Creoles have a similar usage of *done*, and the following two specimens are reported in Jamaican English and rural Guyanese Creole English:

Mi dis [sic] iit *don* ('I just finished eating')
Wen mi kuk *don*, mi a hosl fiid op mi pikni ('When I've finished cooking, I hurry and feed my child')

In these cases, *done* never takes an auxiliary and the verb is in bare infinitive form, not marked for past tense.

The Tristanians make frequent use of completive *done*, but it turns out that their type of *done* cannot be clearly attributed to either of these usages. In Tristan da Cunha English, the most common type is the combination of perfective *be* and *done*, followed by verbs that are sometimes marked for past tense and sometimes not. The local usage would therefore have 'I's done gone and done it', and not 'I done go' or 'I've done gone'. This is puzzling, since by far the most common Middle English type always involved *have*, and the Creole construction never takes an auxiliary. How are we to explain that Tristanians predominantly have completive *done* with the verb *be*? Did one of the settlers bring this combination of features, or did the two merge on the island? To complicate matters, whereas we know that contemporary Saint Helenian English has completive *done*, there is considerable evidence that this feature may have died out in the British Isles, perhaps as early as in the 1600s. Michael Montgomery, who analysed hundreds of English and Scottish manuscripts written between 1600 and 1800, found not a single trace of it, and the last attested form in the literature is from Nicol Burne's 'The Disputation', written in the 1580s. This is important for the development of Tristan da Cunha English. If completive *done* disappeared before 1750, then none of the British settlers on Tristan could have brought it to the island. St Helena has completive *done*, but the little information available suggests that 'I done eat' is much more common than 'I's done eat', and St Helenians, when asked whether and what type of *done* they use, point to the Creole type and say that they have never heard a structure that involves both *done* and an auxiliary. So why would the Tristanians have '*be done*'? Why would they say 'I's done eat my supper', and not what we would expect, 'I done eat my supper' or 'I've done eat my supper'? If completive *done* was a legacy of Saint Helenian English or earlier forms of British English, we would expect that other types were adopted. Therefore, it is not possible to assess whether structures such as 'I's done bake her a cake' represent a remnant form from British English (particularly since an identical combination, "the battle is done ceiss", makes its appearance in John Dunbar's works), or whether they originated in the mixing of two different elements, namely perfective *be* from British donors and completive *done* from Saint Helenian English. In this particular case, completive *done* on Tristan may be either old or new, archaic or dynamic, and we just do not know which.

One final structure we would like to discuss does not represent a legacy of one or several of the founders, but rather an innovation that most likely developed on the island itself. One of the exclusive and community–based innovations is the usage of past marked forms, such as *kept* or *went*, with co-occurring *used to* or *had to*, resulting in sentences like "we never *used to kep'* records in them days" or "we *had to wen'* out for to get firewood". Such usage is unknown elsewhere; people on St Helena told us that they have never heard such structures in their dialect, and nobody has reported these structures in the British Isles. It is thus more than likely that *used to went* does not represent a legacy of donor dialects, but on the contrary, that it was developed by the Tristanians themselves. As it turns out, other speakers of English use similar structures. For instance, Walt Wolfram (1974) studied forms of English as a second language in the Puerto Rican community in New York City, and found that some adolescents, who are fluent and use both English and Spanish in their every-day lives, on occasion say "I didn't meant it", which resembles the Tristanian usage strongly. Therefore, it is quite plausible that *used to went* represents the influence of non–native varieties of English on Tristan da Cunha English. We know from the missionaries' records that the community was English-speaking and that there was thus no direct language contact on the island, and from Peter Green's correspondence we know that he mastered English very well. Nevertheless, Green and/or the other non-

Anglophone settlers may well have used past marked forms with *used to* or *had to*, and the first generations of children may have adopted it from them. In any case, this seems to be a genuinely unique feature, endemic to the local dialect, and the fact that it was maintained from the speech of the Dutch, Danish and/or the Italians is another piece of evidence that allows us to reconstruct the evolution of Tristan da Cunha English.

We also find innovations that concern the sound system of the dialect, such as the pronunciation of words such as *think*, pronounced 'sink', and *throw*, 'srow'. The realisation of the English /th/ and /dh/ sounds (in *thistle* and *this*) are notoriously difficult for learners of English as a foreign language, since the two sounds are unknown in most of the world's languages. Native speakers of German, Spanish or Hindi, for instance, commonly struggle with producing these sounds, and replace them with sounds that come close and are easier to make, for instance /s/ or /t/. One other innovation in Tristan da Cunha English is the insertion of /b/ sounds in words like *flour*, *shower*, and *hour*, which are pronounced 'flubba', 'shubba', and 'hubba'. Visitors to Tristan are often confused when they hear these pronunciations, and a visiting doctor had no idea what his local guide to the mountain was talking about when saying "don't worry, jus' half a hubba". All these features may represent innovations that originated on Tristan da Cunha, and they are quite likely limited to his dialect of English.

To sum things up, we find sounds, words and grammatical structures of British English, that were brought to the island by William Glass and his companions. On the other hand, there exists also a number of features that cannot have been brought to Tristan via the British settlers (either they do not exist in British English, or if they do, they are not found in the areas where the colonisers came from originally). These structures are frequent in St Helenian English and must have been brought via the women from St Helena. Most of these features resemble English-based Creoles (particularly the reduction of word-final consonants and the lack of *–s* attachment with third person singulars, but also the absence of any form of the verb 'to be' in sentences such as 'I hittin' on the win' gonna change' or 'the cattle more wilder Stony Beach'). This suggests that a creolized form of English was spoken by at least some of these women, and that they must have had a considerable impact in the Tristan da Cunha community, both socially and linguistically. The co-occurrence of British, St Helenian as well as totally unique and innovative structures is a strong indication that the dialect developed out of a mixing situation. Tristan da Cunha English is consequently not the equivalent of a single dialect transplanted to the South Atlantic Ocean: the first Tristan-born children selected features from several (or perhaps even all) of the dialects that were brought to the island, and blended them to a unique, innovative and distinctive variety of colonial English. Tristan da Cunha English as it is spoken today had a number of founders, both fathers and mothers alike.

3.5 Where does Tristan da Cunha English go from here?

A last point we would like to discuss concerns the future of the local dialect. As we saw, the community has undergone abrupt transformation in the second half of the 20th century, and the Tristanians are now spending more time than ever away from the island. They often leave the island for secondary education or simply for a vacation, and they are encouraged by the government to get further job training and enhance their professional know–how abroad. Notwithstanding this increase in mobility, the population is stable. Most Tristanians return to their South Atlantic homes once they have made their experiences in the outside world and discovered that the grass is not really greener on the other side. Permanent out–migration is limited, and very few Tristanians turn their back to the island for good and settle elsewhere. The Tristanians have a strong local identity; most of them are happy where they are and would not want to live anywhere else.

The question is, however, the extent to which the changes in the island's social life have an effect on language. What does the future hold for Tristan da Cunha English?

Perhaps the community's increasing mobility will lead to the successive adoption of features of varieties of English spoken elsewhere, causing the local dialect to assimilate to them. This could result in the gradual extinction of the characteristic features of Tristanian English. Is the dialect going to erode as the community emerges from insularity and adapts to the outside world? Is the traditional 'Tristan Slang' disappearing as the Tristanians pick up new dialect forms in South Africa or in the UK? This scenario has been documented in other formerly isolated places, for instance on the island of Ocracoke, one of the Outer Banks islands off the coast of North Carolina.

Ocracoke was fairly isolated until World War II, and the community had few contacts with the mainland and was economically self-sufficient, based on fishing. Then, in the 1950s and 1960s, the island began to open up and is now a popular holiday resort. More and more tourists came to spend their holidays on the Outer Banks, a regular ferry service was established with the mainland and other Outer Banks islands, and today Ocracoke attracts visitors from all parts of the US east coast. Motels, restaurants, bed and breakfast establishments sprang up, along with a range of shops and places of entertainment. As a result, the job market changed, and more and more locals were employed in the tourist industry, coming into contact with ever-increasing numbers of off-islanders. Moreover, hundreds of outsiders retired to the island and now live on Ocracoke permanently, which of course transformed the community's social life. Traditional employment in the fishing industry declined and there are now very few O'Cockers (as they call themselves) who fish for a living. These changes had an impact on the language of the O'Cockers as well, and younger community members have far fewer traditional dialect features (such as an "oi" sound in words like *high* and *tide*; or *weren't* with all persons, as in *it weren't me*) than their parents and grandparents. Ocracoke is thus a pertinent example of the effects of mobility on language change, and the linguistic consequences of economic transformation are so far-reaching that Walt Wolfram and his associates, who studied the dialect, are concerned that the local dialect erodes and warn that is in danger of disappearing altogether.

So what is happening on Tristan da Cunha? Do the Tristanians pick up features of South African, St Helenian or British English, and maintain using them upon their return? The community is much more open now than it was twenty or forty years ago, but still there are not too many visitors on the island, and very few 'station fellas' reside on Tristan da Cunha. So the recent developments are not as drastic and far-reaching as in places like Ocracoke. On the other hand, it is noticeable that younger Tristanians use fewer traditional dialect features than elderly ones. Linguistic analysis also shows that younger and more mobile Tristanians speak somewhat differently than those who hardly ever left the island; they are much less likely to have features such as 'hypercorrect *h*' or completive *done*, or to pronounce *hour* and *flour* as 'hubba' and 'flubba'. While they continue to use these features, they use them less often than their parents and grandparents, or their peers who have never been to the outside world. This would therefore suggest that, as has been documented in other locales, traditional forms will die out within a couple of generations if this trend continues.

On the other hand, we need to be cautious when making such predictions. Language transforms constantly, and change only stops once a language ceases to be spoken (which happened in the case of Latin, for example). All language varieties, no matter how isolated or integrated they are, are constantly in a state of flux and variation. We do not know how elderly Tristanians spoke when they were in their teens; the changes we hear in younger speakers may not be permanent and it is possible that more traditional features increase again at a later stage in their lives. Another important point concerns the fact that younger Tristanians may have become more aware of the appropriateness of when to use their local dialect and when to use a more 'outside-world' type of English. Younger Tristanians are highly aware of their distinctive usage and comment on it frequently. The possibility exists that more mobile members of the community continue to speak the local dialect with their families and friends, but that they switch when communicating with outsiders, speaking a dialect that more closely resembles British or South African English.

Increasing mobility might therefore lead to the usage of two forms of the dialect, the 'Tristan Slang' used within the community, and a more mainstream dialect with foreigners and visitors. Since all the recordings that were subject to linguistic analysis so far were conducted by outsiders, there is the risk that different language usage is misinterpreted as dialect erosion, whereas in fact it represents nothing else than an acute sense of when and with whom to speak Tristan da Cunha English and when and with whom not. To give but one example, Daniel Schreier recorded about two and a half hours of natural conversation with two younger Tristanians who had spent years abroad for further education. In the presence of a "station fella" and a tape recorder, they did not use a single form of completive *done*, which at first sight seems a strong indication that they do not use this feature at all. Then, however, Schreier noticed that, when the recorder was switched off and other Tristanians were around, the very same speakers used completive *done* quite a lot, in fact so much that he started to write down examples every time he heard one in their speech. In the end, he came up with more than 50 examples, which he collected in two afternoons only. The interpretation of the recording, namely that Tristan da Cunha English is dying out, could thus not be further from the truth. In this case, at least, it is obvious that Tristanian features are mostly used when Tristanians are among themselves and less frequently when they are with outsiders, or interviewed for the purpose of dialect research.

This is therefore not the most satisfying answer we can give, but we just cannot be sure whether Tristan da Cunha English is really disappearing or not. The best we can do for now is to monitor language changes in the generations to come, and perhaps use a local fieldworker who could conduct interviews so that we can compare the speech of different generations and find out if and how much Tristanians alter their dialect. This may enable us to find out if the Tristanians are in the process of becoming bi-dialectal, speaking their local dialect at home and a different, more "international" kind of English with people who are not members of the community. It is perhaps also too early to tell, since off–island education and job training only started some 20 years ago, but we will definitely keep an eye on the community and may have an answer to this question within the next one or two generations. What is certain is that the dialect is strongly associated with the life-style and culture of the Tristan da Cunha community. Regardless of age and mobility, the Tristanians have a strong local identity. Many of them are aware that their dialect reflects the rich and unique settlement history of their ancestors and would feel a sense of loss if the traditional form of Tristan da Cunha English disappeared.

Faces of Tristan

Above left: Daphne and Ernie Repetto outside their home

Left: Herbert Glass, fisherman and head carpenter

Below left: Mark Swain, sailing to Nightingale

Above right: Robin Repetto and his daughter Jade

Below right: Natalie Swain and Janine Lavarello

Gary Repetto

Cynthia Green

Graham Rogers

The newly-born Randel Repetto
with his grandmother, Joyce Hagan

Kaitlyn, Julia, and Karl Hagan

Marie Repetto and
Karen Lavarello-Schreier

71

Epilogue

Our portrait of the community has aimed at integrating both contemporary and historical facets of life on Tristan da Cunha. In our view, it is remarkable how the Tristanians have continuously adapted to the outside world, and how they face up to the challenges of the 21st century, while preserving their cultural heritage and traditions. From the 1885 lifeboat disaster, the total isolation during WWI, and the occupation of their island in 1942 to the volcanic eruption and the two years in English exile, the Tristanians constantly had to take on new challenges while respecting their own history and culture.

Recently, their lives have experienced another setback. On May 21st 2001, the island was hit by what can only be described as a "perfect storm". Tristan da Cunha, dangerously close to the "Roaring Forties", the southernmost part of the Atlantic, has always faced harsh weather conditions and tempestuous gales. However, the hurricane that hit the island on that fateful day is unparalleled in living memory; not even Gertie Lavarello, the oldest member of the community, could remember such a powerful natural disaster. The destruction was so immense that the islanders were unable to contact the outside world, and the extent of the destruction emerged only when radio and satellite contact was re-established with the UK in early June. Immediately after the storm, James Glass, the Chief Islander and official representative of the community, wrote a harrowing account of the events and kindly gave us permission to reprint it here:

> "With autumn closing, everyone was preparing for a wet winter. Two weeks previously one gale had come and torn off an islander's roof, in such a way no one had experienced, but worse was to follow on Monday the 21st May. It was a grey murky morning, overcast and raining with a stiff breeze. Work started in the normal way, but around 9.00 am the wind started to increase from the Southeast, the sea started to become a continuous whirlwind of white water, and by 11.00 am a ferocious storm struck the island. All Heads of the various Government Departments were informed to let their staff stop work and return to their homes as the wind continued to become stronger and the asbestos roofing was starting to blow off various Government Department buildings.

The storage section of the fishing factory after it was ravaged by the hurricane

People could be seen running from one building to another, for shelter, helping each other to secure their doors and roofs often blown off their feet, to avoid the flying debris (mostly asbestos) which could easily have decapitated people before being blown clean off the Island into the sea. The fish factory freezer was lifted from its foundation and thrown 20m up the road, and a quarter of the fishing factory roof was damaged or taken completely off.

At approximately 12:30 p.m. all men were asked to assemble at the hospital to try and salvage the hospital equipment, and prevent any more of the roof to be blown off. Ropes were thrown over the roof and tied down, but nothing else could be done due to the force of wind and rain, which pelted into ones face like pins horizontally. The gable end of the hospital collapsed and a quarter of the hospital was blown down, losing the theatre and x–ray room.

The roof of the operation and X-ray room of the local hospital was blown off and all technical facilities were ruined

Tremendous damage was done to the Prince Philip Hall, the only community centre, and Pub (The Albatross Bar) on the island. The sheets of asbestos roofing and overhead verandas were torn from the back and front of Prince Philip Hall, the loft of the main dance hall fell in and the whole building became waterlogged. Three of the Tristan longboats, unique to Tristan and secured by metal spikes in the ground outside of the Residency garden, were lifted and tossed into the garden, with one being lifted through the air sixty metres and deposited in the Rectory's back garden, demolishing a potato shed.

Several Tristan longboats, firmly fastened to the ground, were lifted and tossed across a stone wall, one as far as 60 metres

Power cables were blown down and scattered the village like a tangled fishing net. That night the inhabitants of Edinburgh settlement sheltered nervously in the dark or in candlelight, some in inches deep water, others in neighbours' homes. The majority of the community sat up all night, wondering if their roof was going to be the next to be ripped off, or waiting for the call of a neighbour to help. Comments made by the eldest pensioner on the island, aged ninety–four, were that she had never heard weather like that since her birth. The wind, screeching and howling, became quite deafening at times.

With all lines down and the 100ft Jaguar, although held by eighteen steel cables listed over, the island was totally cut of from the outside world. A number of roofing sheets had blown off the radio shack, and when the window blew in it sucked the mobile sat phone out, and the rest of the radio equipment became waterlogged. However, there was a spare one and with this the following day the Acting Administrator called the FCO to inform them that Tristan would be out of contact until the electricity supply could be restored. One of the satellite dishes just installed a few months ago was totally demolished and ripped off the mounting.

The day after the storm, despite wind and rain, the islanders systematically worked on the houses which roofs had blown off, whilst the women helped one another dry out flooded rooms and passages. They worked all day and before dusk that night all Islanders' houses roofs bad been replaced. Thanks to the efficiency of the electricians on the island a temporary line was installed from the Factory. The following day the Administration office was back in operation, but the village remained without electricity for six days. Whilst the islanders cleaned up the village, the same force of wind and rain came from the West hitting the potato patches four miles to the west, again causing great damage. Camping huts' roofs and as many as twenty seed sheds to the west of the settlement which holds next years crop were blown away and seed damaged, probably affecting next year's potato crops, which could be disastrous. For the last six days all islanders worked in oilskin suits from dusk till dawn to restore the damage, and to secure what could not be rebuilt until funds and supplies became available. It is not yet known how many cattle died in this storm, but the figure at the moment is thirty and continues to rise. The loss to the Island sheep flocks is unknown but thought to be considerable, and this is only on the settlement plain. As yet the weather has not allowed us to visit the back of the Island or the Islands of Nightingale and Inaccessible. The roofing was torn from the Anglican Church Vestry and the Tower Bell blown down, but it did not deter the islanders, for on Sunday morning (27th May) both churches were packed, to give thanks that no serious injury or loss of life took place amongst the islanders. The electricians then switched on the village electricity supply and checked every house on the island. That night for most of us life was back to almost normal.

It is common knowledge that most islanders are not well off, the average wage for Government employees on Tristan is £152.34 per month. The after–effects of the storm will cost much hardship as families try and restore their properties and possessions. A local Disaster Fund has been set up to help those less fortunate, and Community spirit is stronger than ever. The island has no Insurance Company, no source of reserve and help is desperately needed to ease the financial loss. Despite the loss and damage done, the most important thing is that we can thank God that no one was hurt during this storm. The sun shines and half of the Union Jack still flies on the remotest Island of Tristan da Cunha."

In almost two centuries of settlement, the Tristanians have always had to face and battle the elements. They have survived severe storms and gales up to 140 km per hour; they made it through food shortages, tidal waves, lifeboat disasters and volcanic eruptions.

There is no question that they will survive the 2001 hurricane also. They immediately set out to work hard and restore the island as it was, and the island is about to return to normality and daily routine. At the same time, James Glass describes the desperate situation of the community. The Tristanians are skilled and hard–working people, but the effects of the hurricane were so disastrous that it is simply impossible for them to repair all the damage by themselves. They need whatever help they can possibly get in their efforts to restore what the storm destroyed. Industry and hard work alone are not enough to return to normal life without amassing catastrophic debt. The present book is our contribution to assist the Tristanians in their efforts, and we donate all our authors' royalties to the disaster fund and those in need.

The remains of the islanders' shacks on Nightingale Island

Meanwhile, the hurricane lives on in the memories of those who lived to see it and witnessed its power. Time will tell whether May 21st 2001 goes down as the "Day of the Hurricane", just as the period 1961-63 is still known as the "Volcano Years". What is certain is that the Tristan community is united and strong, and determined to master whatever challenge it is facing. To the Tristanians, there is no place like home and their home is Tristan. But it will take money as well as dedication to get their island home back to its former state.

A Tristan Glossary[1]

Appling days Traditional custom whereby the entire community sailed to Sandy Point to collect apples and other fruit. This tradition has been abandoned in recent years, primarily due to Tristan's economic transformation (see p 40).

Bakki Pick-up truck (< Afrikaans).

Bawling [bɔːlən] Lowing of a cow. (Dialectal English *bawl* 'to low as a cow', attested in diverse locations, EDD.)

Berry time Season when the ripe ***island berries*** are gathered (February-March).

Billy Ram (as in British English *billy*-goat).

Blinders [blaɪndəs] Hazardous rocks under the surface of the ocean.

Bluefish Local fish species, *Seriolella antarctica*, which takes its name from the bluish colour of its back and head.

Bluestone Local stone traditionally used for building purposes.

Bluff The Bluff is a cliff with a broad front which marks the southern end of the Settlement plain, immediately south of the ***patches*** (see p 37).

Dog fern A tree fern, *Blechnum palmiforme*, which grows up to one metre in height.

Braai [braɪ] Barbecue (< Afrikaans).

Brady [breɪdi] Fried meat (usually beef) cooked with added vegetables (e.g. cabbage *brady*, pumpkin *brady*, etc; < Afrikaans *bredie*).

Brother Term of address between well acquainted men (cf ***buddy***).

Bubble up Increase (of the swell in the ocean), e.g. *the sea **bubbled up** real fas'*.

Buddy Term of address between well acquainted men (cf *brother*). (Although generally considered as an Americanism, this term is first attested in the Creole English of St Kitts in the Caribbean in 1785 (Baker 1999:324).)

Bullplace Slaughterhouse.

Bully beef Boiled beef. (***Bully*** derives from French *bouilli* 'boiled'. In British English, *bully beef* refers specifically to tinned beef which became well known through its use as army rations in the Franco-Prussian War of 1870-71.)

Bully hash Dish made with ***bully beef*** and potatoes.

Bulting Spading. (No origin for this term has yet been found.)

Bunkatina Bench. (Precise origin unknown, but clearly related to ***bunky***.)

Bunky Stool, small bench (< Afrikaans *bankie* 'bench').

Canary The Tristan bunting, *Nesospiza acunhae*, whose primary habitat is Nightingale Island (see p 61).

Canteen The name given to Tristan's one and only local supermarket (see pp 61-62 for details).

Carding gang Party of women carding and spinning wool.

Catfish Octopus (see p 61 for details).

Chesty Short of breath, wheezy, particularly caused by asthma (which is common in Tristan, see *hashmere*).

Concha Local fish species, *Labrichthys ornatus*. (Origin unknown.)

Cool drink Soda, soft drink. (***Cool drink*** is similarly used in India and some other Asian countries.)

Cooler Refrigerator (see p 61).

Crawfish Tristan spiny lobster, *Jasus tristani*. (In Britain, the spiny lobster is sometimes termed 'crayfish'. ***Crawfish*** is the American English word corresponding to British English *crayfish*.)

Crawford Curious, inquisitive person (*you's an old **Crawford***). This presumably refers to Allan Crawford, the British cartographer who visited the island in the

---

[1] Abbreviations used in the glossary are: EDD = *English Dialect Dictionary*, OED = *Oxford English Dictionary*, SDD = *Scots Dialect Dictionary*, SOED = *Shorter Oxford English Dictionary*.

	1930s and 1940s and who later founded the Tristan da Cunha Association (see p 20).
Diceling	[daɪslən] Thistle (see p 60). (< Dialectal English, cf *dicel* [daɪsl] 'thistle', attested in Devon and Cornwall - EDD. The word is wrongly glossed as 'a dock plant' in Zettersten 1969.)
Docks	Dock, a weed often found in the potato patches.
Dog catcher	Type of weed with clingy burrs.
Dong	Empty gas bottle, used as an alarm signal and to announce a fishing day.
Donkey dance	Traditional Tristan dance, in which pairs of dancers move around in circles,imitating a trotting and then a galloping donkey. Like the *pillow dance*, this is one of the great traditional dances, accompanied by a tune on the accordion (see p 25), and used to be performed at every social gathering. It is still occasionally performed although nowadays very few Tristanians know how to play the tune.
Duff-head	Cow without horns.
East	Clockwise around the island, starting at the settlement (often used instead of 'right'); cf *west*.
Egg trip	A trip to neighbouring Nightingale Island for the purpose of collecting penguin eggs, a local delicacy (see p 46).
Fake out	Worn out, tired.
Fanny's tea	Drink consisting of half boiling water and half milk.
Fardi	Godfather.
Fivefinger	Local fish species, *Acantholatris monodactylus*, with prominent dark stripes on its sides. See p 61.
For to	In order to, e.g. *the captain tell us **for to** steer west.* (This is widely attested in dialectal British and overseas varieties of English.)
Fresh	Lacking in salt.
Frig	Deceive, fool, e.g. *you half **frigged** me* 'you really fooled me'.
Gansey	Knitted pullover (cf English *guernsey* 'a thick, knitted, closely fitting vest or shirt (...) worn by seamen', SOED).
Gony	Tristan wandering albatross, *Diomedea (exulans) dabbenena*. (Origin unknown.)
Green load of wood on you	Drunk.
Guess	Reckon, assume. (This is far more common in American than in British English and may reflect the influence of American settlers.)
Gulch	Steep, narrow ravine (common in American English, reflecting the influence of American settlers).
Gully	Small gulch
Gutter	Narrow ravine covered with grass.
H	The *h* sound is frequently inserted before words which start with a stressed vowel is English, as in *hadichock, hadmin,* and *hashmere* below. (See also pp 62-63).
Hadichock	Small, inedible potato (< *artichoke*).
Hadmin	Administrator
Hairy fella	A young petrel that does not yet have feathers.
Haish	[haɪʃ] Exclamation meaning 'go on' (to animals).
Half	Quite, e.g. *I's **half** tired* 'I'm quite tired'. (Perhaps from colloquial British English *not half*, as in *I'm not half hungry* 'I'm very hungry'.)
Hallion	Halyard.
Hangchers	Often colourful headscarf, traditionally worn by women. (This derives from the now obsolete English *handkercher* 'headscarf' or 'handkerchief'.)
Hardies	A prominent rock formation in the sea, to the west of the Settlement, just off the potato *patches*, traditionally used for navigation purposes.
Hashmere	Asthma.

Hatchabali	Exclamation to frighten children (often reduced to **hatcha**). (Origin unknown.)
Haul out	To change (of the weather and/or wind), e.g. *the wind has **haul out***.
Heis	[haɪs] Exclamation (probably a euphemism for 'Christ').
Heish up	[haɪʃ ʌp] To hoist.
Heitamassie	[haɪtamasi] Exclamation of astonishment. (Origin unknown.)
Henry	See **Red Henry**.
Heyen on	[haɪjən ɔn] 1. Go on about, talk incessantly about, e.g. *She's **heyen on** her tater cakes* 'She keeps going on about her potato cakes'; 2. Be in for, be due for, e.g. *You's **heyen on** a clip behind the ear* 'you're asking for a clip behind the ear'. (Perhaps from English *eyeing on*.)
-ing	Tristanians usually pronounce English words ending in –ing [ɪŋ] as –en [ən].
is	Are, e.g. *How you **is**?* 'How are you?'.
Island berry	A bush (*Empetrum rubrum*) which produces red berries which are gathered at **berry time**.
Island cock	The Inaccessible rail, *Atlantisia rogersi*, which is confined to that island and is the world's smallest flightless bird (see p 49).
Island tree	*Phylica arborea*, a palm-shaped plant which grows up to 2 metres high.
Jadda boys	Penguin eggs. (Origin unknown. The second element might conceivably be *buoys* rather than *boys*.)
Jais	[dʒeɪs] Exclamation (which rhymes with 'chase'), probably a euphemistic form for *Jesus*.
Jinny	Female donkey, cf English *Jenny-ass*.
Joebucky	Adjective applied to potatoes that are insufficiently cooked and still a bit hard.
Kappi	Bonnet. (Afrikaans *kappi*.)
Kee-kee	[kiki] Ear. (Origin unknown. Widely believed by Tristanians to be from Afrikaans or Dutch but no likely source of this has yet been identified.)
King bird	Tristan tern, *Sterna (vittata) tristanensis*.
Klipfish	[klɪfɪʃ] Local fish species, *Bovichthys diacanthus*. (There are two possible origins for this word, neither of them entirely satisfactory – Danish *klipfisk* and Afrikaans *klipvis*. The Danish (originally Norwegian) word refers to dried cod. *Klip* here corresponds to English 'clip' and relates to the fact that the cod is cut up in pieces before being dried. Dried cod of this kind is known in Canada and some other English-speaking countries as *klipfish*. The Afrikaans word originally designated various small, coral-dwelling fish species – too small to be caught for human consumption. In this case, *klip* means 'rock' (related to English 'cliff') and refers to the locations in which such fish are found. Later, dried cod of the Scandinavian kind became known in South Africa and the same word, *klipvis*, was applied to this. Given that the Tristan **klipfish** is eaten by Tristanians (although considered an inferior to many other species) and is not currently cut into pieces and dried, it does not correspond very closely to the original meanings of either Danish *klipfisk* or Afrikaans *klipvis*. Further historical research may be able to establish which of these two origins is the more likely.)
Kooibietjie	[koɪbitʃi] Take a little nap, sleep for a little while. (Afrikaans *kooi* 'bed' and *bietjie* 'a little bit').
Kraal	Sheep pen (< Afrikaans).
Lekker	Delicious. (This word can also have the meaning of 'attractive', e.g. *Heitamassie, you come in really lekker*, 'Wow! You're looking really good'.) (Afrikaans and/or Dutch *lekker*.)
Longboat	Traditional sailing boat, covered with canvas (see pp 42-43).

Mad	Angry. (This sense is more common in US than in UK English, perhaps reflecting the influence of American settlers.)
Mary	Chrysalis.
Mato sauce	[mʌdi sɔːs] Tomato sauce, tomato ketchup.
Mocans	Moccassins
Molly	Yellow-nosed albatross, *Thalassarche melanophrys*, pictured on page 46. This is an abbreviation of ***mollymawk***, an anglicization of Dutch *mallemok* 'albatross'.
Mollymawk	See **Molly.**
Muddish	Godmother.
Mutton bird	The black eaglet, *Pterodroma macroptera*, a species of petrel.
Nightbird	Broad-billed whalebird, *Dachyptila vittata*, found in abundance on all the islands
Noar	Oar (< English *an oar*, misinterpreted as *a noar*).
Okalolies	[oʊkəloʊliːz] Local tradition of dressing up in disguise on New Years' Eve (perhaps a deformation of Afrikaans *Olie Kolonies* 'old ugly men', see p 40).
Ol' hands	Forefathers of today's population
Ol' Soney	Bogeyman (normally used to scare children, e.g. *be quiet, or **Ol' Soney** gonna come*).
Orchard	Sheltered gully with fruit trees.
Oukabaatjie	[oʊkəbatʃi] Person of racially mixed descent (Afrikaans *ou kabaatjie* 'bogeyman').
Over the keek	Drunk.
Padre	Priest. (This originally Portuguese word is also found in Indian English, British Army usage, and many English-based Creoles.)
Patches	Potato fields and gardens to the west of the Settlement.
Pediunker	Great grey petrel (*Procellaria cinerea*). (Of unknown origin.)
Peeoo	Sooty albatross, *Phoebetria fusca*. (The name is an onomatopoeic imitation of the bird's distinctive call.)
Petrel	Great shearwater. *Puffinus gravis*.
Piccaninny	Child. (This ultimately Portuguese word is attested in practically all English-based Pidgins and Creoles.)
Pickish	Hungry (English *peckish*).
Pillow dance	Traditional Tristan dance, where people move around the dance hall in single file, with a pillow in their hand, enticing others of the opposite sex to give them a kiss, take the pillow and continue the dance. Like the ***donkey dance***, this dance was one of the great traditional dances, accompanied by a particular tune on the accordion (see p 25), and performed at almost every social gathering. It is still performed, even though very few Tristanians know how to play the tune nowadays.
Pinnamin	Penguin. (Of unknown origin.)
Plony	Small sausage; the plural form is ***plonies***. (Probably from English *polony*, a sausage made of pre-cooked meat, the name of which is thought to derive ultimately from *Bologna*, the Italian city.)
Point	To set course for, e.g. *the longboat was **pointin'** straight for Nightingale.*
Puttin' in	Planting potatoes.
Qualmish	[kwɔmiʃ] Word applied to various stomach disorders, see p 52.
Quarter deck	Open area behind the ***canteen*** (formerly part of the ***station*** facilities).
Ratting day	Traditional day when the entire male population hunts rats, a tradition which dates back to the early 1880s when rates came shore from the wreck of the *H B Paul* (see p 40).
Red Henry	Red centipede with a slightly poisonous bite. (The name is often abbreviated to ***Henry***.) Zettersten (1969), citing Barrow (1910), lists this as *Red Harry* but this latter name is not used on Tristan today.)

Road	Outside the Settlement, *road* often means 'path'. (The *west road* on Nightingale Island is a path cut through the **tussock**.)
Rockhopper	A species of penguin, *Eudyptes chrysocome*. See photograph on p 46.
Sailor caps	Dessert made of grated and deep-fried potatoes.
Scouse	Drink consisting of milk and egg yolk. In Britain, *scouse* is the name of a not very nutritious, sailor's stew containing a small amount of meat. (Perhaps the rather different Tristan ingredients date from the early days of settlement when meat was scarce.)
Scratching	Carding wool
Scudda buddy ya	Drunk, tipsy. (Cf Scots *scud* 'to drink copious draughts' EDD.)
Sea-hen	Southern skua, *Catharactes antarctica hamiltoni*.
Shack	The type of housing facilities Tristanians have on Nightingale Island. (This contrasts with their houses in the Settlement and the huts they have in the potato patches area and on the Caves and Stonyhill Plain). There are two types – sleeping shacks and cooking shacks (see p 45). (< North American English, first attested in the latter in 1882 OED.)
Sharing	Dividing of food, common goods, etc..
Sing out	To holler or shout. (This is not unknown in British English, but is particularly common in Australian English and in English Pidgins and Creoles in the Pacific.)
Skip-Jack	White-faced storm petrel, *Pelagodroma marina*.
Skittery arse	A person seeking attention, a show-off. (Cf English *skittish* 'unduly lively or spirited' SOED.)
Smash	Mashed potatoes. (*Smash* has been the leading brand of instant mashed potato in Britain since the 1960s and this term may have been acquired by Tristanians exiled there during the Volcano Years.)
Smoothskin	A small variety of potato.
Snislens	Dessert consisting of fried triangles of dough served with jam. (Cf Scots *snisle* 'to singe, burn partially, harden with heat' EDD.)
Snoek	[snʊk] Local fish species, *Thyrsites atun*. (< Afrikaans or Dutch *snoek* 'pike'.)
Soft stone	Soft volcanic stone, traditionally used for building purposes
Soldier	Small, local fish species, red and orange in colour, *Sebastichys capensis*.
Sot	[sɔt] Seat across the longboat (?< English *athwart*).
Spading	Digging of the **patches**. (Dialectal English *spade* 'to dig with a spade' EDD.)
Spell	Rest, nap. (This word is also found in this sense in Australian English.)
Spotty dick	Dessert closely resembling the one known in British English as *spotted dick* (see p 50).
Starchy	The Tristan thrush, *Nesocichla eremita*.
Station	Facilities of the naval garrison, stationed on the island during WWII.
Station fella	Expatriate staying on the island (see p 4).
Steenbras	[stiːnbras] Local fish species (< Dutch *steenbras*, 'stone bream').
Stinker	Giant fulmar, *Macronectes giganteus*. This sea bird is also common in South Africa. (The first syllable of the English word fulmar derives from an Old Norse word for 'stinking'.)
Stop	Live, stay with. (See p 61. This usage is very common in English-based Pidgins and Creoles.)
Stumpnose	A local (and possibly endemic) fish species, *Seriolella christopherseni*. It grows up to two metres long, and was discovered by Erling Christophersen, the leader of the 1937 Norwegian Expedition (see p 47).
Suckies	Flax sticks.
Tackies	Running shoes (also found in South African English).
Tailing	Cutting off the crawfish tails before processing.
Taters	Potatoes. (Common in colloquial American English.)

Teem   Pour out, e.g. *teem me out a gin and tonic.* (This sense is attested in many different British locations by the EDD although it appears to be rare today.)

Three sheets to the wind   Drunk. (This expression is common in colloquial British English.)

Tiddy   Sister, female friend, term of endearment between women, e.g. *How you is, tiddy?* (Cf Scots *titty* 'a child's word for sister' SDD.)

Tier   Four rows in a *patch.*

Tired   Out of breath (usually because of asthma).

Tissick   Mild bronchitis. (< English *phthisic* [tɪzɪk] (adjective relating to) 'a wasting disease of the lungs; pulmonary consumption' SOED.)

Touch up   Drunk, tipsy, e.g. *your tiddy is half touch up* 'your (female) friend is very drunk'.

Tristan pudding   Suet pudding with berries or raisins.

Try out   Extract oil from blubber by frying in a pan. (Cf dialectal English *try* 'melt or boil down lard in order to purify it' EDD.)

Tussock   Tall grass, up to 8 feet in height (*Spartina arundinacea*), which once covered the entire settlement plain of Tristan and still abounds on the neighbouring islands.

Volcano Years   The two-year period in English exile, following the eruption of the volcano in August 1961 (see p 22-26).

Wait on   Wait for. (This is very common in Scottish English).

Watren   [wɔtrɛn] Small stream. (< English *watering*).

Wee   Small. (This is the normal Scots word for 'small'.)

West   Anti-clockwise around the island, starting at the settlement (often used instead of 'left'). Cf *east.*

Whiteblossom   A variety of potato.

Worming   Removing the guts of crawfish before processing.

Y'all   Second person plural form of 'you' (*Where y'all going?*), also found in Southern US American English

Yard   Small enclosure, surrounded by walls. Very often this refers to a vegetable garden or a potato patch.

Yellowtail   Species of Cape mackerel, *Seriola lalandii.*

References

Baker, Philip 1999 Investigating the origin and diffusion of shared features among the Atlantic English Creoles. Baker, Philip & Bruyn, Adrienne (eds) *St Kitts and the Atlantic Creoles*. London: University of Westminster Press 315-64.

Barrow, K M 1910 *Three years in Tristan da Cunha*. London: Skeffington.

Beintema, Albert <http://home.wxs.nl/~beintema/ships.htm>.

Booy, Daniel M 1957 *Rock of exile – a narrative of Tristan da Cunha*. London: J M Dent & Sons.

Brander, Jan 1940 *Tristan da Cunha 1506 – 1902*. London: Allen &Unwin.

Christophersen, E 1940 *Tristan da Cunha, the lonely isle*. London: Cassell.

Crabb, George 1980 *The history and postal history of Tristan da Cunha*. Self-published manuscript.

Crawford, Allan 1941 *I went to Tristan*. London: Allen & Unwin.

—— 1982 *Tristan da Cunha and the Roaring Forties*. London: Allen & Unwin.

—— 1999 *Penguins, potatoes, and postage stamps. A Tristan da Cunha chronicle*. Oswestry: Anthony Nelson.

Doveton, Miss 1881 A sketch abroad. Oliver, S P *On board a Union steamer*. London: W H Allen, 1881, 227-73

Earle, Augustus 1966 *Narrative of a residence on the island of Tristan D'Acunha in the South Atlantic Ocean*. Oxford: Clarendon Press (1st edn 1832).

Evans, Dorothy 1994 *Schooling in the South Atlantic Islands 1661–1992*. Oswestry: Anthony Nelson.

Falk–Rønne, Arne 1967 *Back to Tristan*. London: Allen & Unwin.

Gane, Douglas M 1932 *Tristan da Cunha. An empire outpost and its keepers with glimpses of its past and considerations of the future*. London: Allen & Unwin.

Hancock, Ian F 1991 St Helena English. Byrne, Francis & Huebner, Thom (ed.) *Development and structures of Creole languages*, Amsterdam: Benjamins, 17-28.

Holdgate, Martin 1958 *Mountains in the sea*. London: Macmillan.

Hosegood, Nancy 1974 *The Glass island*. London: Hodder & Stoughton.

Lajolo, Anna & Lombardi, Guido 1999 *Tristan da Cunha: l'isola leggendaria / Tristan da Cunha: the legendary island*. Chiavari (Genoa): Museo Marinaro Tommasino-Andreatta.

Little, W, Fowler, H W, & Coulson, J 1973 *The Shorter Oxford English Dictionary*. Oxford: Oxford University Press, 3rd edition.

Lockhart, John G 1933 *Blenden Hall*. London: Appleton.

Mackay, Margaret 1963 *The angry island: The story of Tristan da Cunha 1506 – 1963*. London: Barker.

Montgomery, Michael 1989 Exploring the roots of Appalachian English. *English World-Wide* 10:2 227-78.

—— 1998. In the Appalachians they speak like Shakespeare. Bauer, L & Trudgill, P (eds.). *Language Myths*. London: Penguin Books.

Mothers' Union 1999 *Recipe Book*. Tristan da Cunha: St Mary's Church.

Munch, Peter A 1945 *Sociology of Tristan da Cunha*. Oslo: Det Norske Videnskaps Akademi.

—— 1971 *Crisis in Utopia*. London: Longman.

Reinecke, John E 1937 Marginal languages. Unpublished PhD thesis, Yale University.

Rogers, Rose 1925 *The lonely island*. London: Allen & Unwin.

Rubin, Jeff 1996 *Antarctica. A Lonely Planet travel survival kit*. Hawthorne, Australia: Lonely Planet Publications.

Schilling-Estes, Natalie 2002 On the nature of isolated and post-isolated dialects. Innovation, variation, and differentiation. *Journal of Sociolinguistics* 6:64-85.

Schreier, Daniel 2003 *Isolation and language change: Contemporary and sociohistorical evidence from Tristan da Cunha English.* Houndmills (Basingstoke) & New York: Palgrave Macmillan.

Simpson, S A & Weiner, E S C 1989 *The Oxford English Dictionary.* Oxford: Oxford University Press, 2nd edition.

Taylor, William F 1856 *Some account of the settlement of Tristan d'Acunha in the South Atlantic Ocean.* London: Cassell.

Warwick, Alexander & Grant, William 1911 *A Scots dialect dictionary.* London & Edinburgh: W & R Chambers.

Wolfram, Walt 1974 *Sociolinguistic aspects of assimilation: Puerto Rican English in New York City.* Washington, DC: Center for Applied Linguistics.

—— 1996 Delineation and description in dialectology: The case of perfective *I'm* in Lumbee English. *American Speech* 71:5-26.

Wolfram, Walt & Schilling-Estes, Natalie 1995 Moribund dialects and the language endangerment canon: The Case of the Ocracoke Brogue. *Language* 71:696-721.

—— & —— 1997 *Hoi Toide on the Outer Banks: the story of the Ocracoke Brogue.* Chapel Hill: The University of North Carolina Press.

Zettersten, Arne 1969 *The English of Tristan da Cunha.* Lund: Gleerup.

Useful websites and additional information

The official Tristan da Cunha website is:
<http://website.lineone.net/~sthelena/tristaninfo.htm>.

Other recommended websites are:
<http://home.planet.nl/~beintema/ships.htm>
<http://www.btinternet.com/~sa_sa/tristan_da_cunha/annals_main.html>
<http://www.btinternet.com/~sa_sa/tristan_da_cunha/tristan_history.html>
<http://www.ndsu.nodak.edu/subantarctic/tristan_da_cunha_group_and_gough.htm>

The following website gives information on the flora and fauna of Tristan da Cunha:
<http://www.jncc.gov.uk/international/pdf/Tristan%20da%20C.pdf>

For those who wish to make contact with others interested in Tristan:
<http://groups.yahoo.com/group/tristan-da-cunha/>

For information on the Tristan da Cunha Association, contact:
Michael Swales, FRGS
c/o Denstone College
Uttoxeter,
Staffordshire ST14 5HN
England
<http://www.tristanassociation.org.uk/>
e-mail <email@tristanassociation.org.uk>

The Peter A Munch/Tristan da Cunha Collection
The world's most extensive collection of documents, film, photos and artifacts on Tristan da Cunha is housed in the archives of Pius XII Memorial Library at Saint Louis University, St Louis, Missouri, USA. The core of the holdings, the Peter A Munch/Tristan da Cunha Collection, is a gift of Helene Munch, widow of the creator of the collection, which includes field notes and manuscripts by Munch, correspondence, scholarly papers, clippings, copies of documents and published materials regarding Tristan, as well as ephemera and personal and financial records. Although the material constitutes an extensive summary of Tristan history and culture from its discovery to the mid-1980s (when Munch passed away), the bulk of the collection dates from 1937 (the Norwegian Expedition to Tristan da Cunha, of which Munch was a member, see pp 19-20) to 1970, roughly Munch's years of professional involvement with Tristan. This collection also documents Munch's own research into the relationship between culture and personality as he observed it among the Tristan islanders. Two other related Tristan collections in the Archives are those of Charles E Marske, student of Professor Munch and now sociology professor at Saint Louis University, and of Samuel P Eastman, a Canadian collector of Tristan research. Descriptions of these collections are now available through the Saint Louis University website, at:
<http://www.slu.edu/libraries/pius/archives/indexpage.html>.

For more information on the language of Tristan da Cunha, contact Daniel Schreier at:
<daniel.schreier@sprachlit.uni-regensburg.de>.

Index
(including explanations of abbreviations used in the text)